FOUND MYSELF
at a FARM

a memoir

SONIA LOPEZ

DENVER, COLORADO

http://www.outskirtspress.com

ISBN: 978-1-4787-4350-7

Outskirts Press and the "OP" logo are trademarks belonging to Outskirts Press, Inc.

PRINTED IN THE UNITED STATES OF AMERICA

Dedication

Like water carves its way through rock to follow its path, so must emotion and words unsaid find an outlet and bleed their way on to paper. There they lay in wait, hoping for a future day in which to reach the heart.

I wrote this for my children, so that in a future day when I am no longer here I may still speak to them with the words I left behind and you may know how much I loved you. May you find strength and courage from my struggle. May you always look forward to a bright tomorrow and be grateful for all you have, for you have more than you know. To my friends and Family, you are what color my world and the music that puts a spring in my steps. And to Mrs. Edwina Fleming for letting me share in her dream, I will be forever grateful.

෴ ෴

Photo credits
Karenina Hilen Photography
Olliver Willis Fleming
Edwina Willis Fleming

Table of Contents

The arrival

*I*t was late at night. I was sitting on the floor in the stall with Tiger's head in my lap. I smelled the sweetness of the freshly laid hay I had put out in preparation for the awaited arrival. She had been in labor all afternoon, she would stretch out her back and paw the floor in pain, walk around looking for a good spot to lie. You could tell when a contraction was coming. She would raise her tail, arch her back and look straight ahead, as if in a trance. I wanted to help her but, did not know what else to do. My employer and I had visited a farm nearby that had goats. She was an English lady with a profound love of animals. She had purchased the land and had a dream of turning it into a self-sustaining farm, with all kinds of animals. I think she wanted to recreate an English country side with sheep and goats dotting the landscape. We purchased five goats and brought them home, six months ago. When we visited the farm it was kidding season and there were baby goats everywhere. They were all kinds of colors. They were running around playing and jumping. We had to have some. We brought home three girls and two boys; Diana, Millie, and Tiger. Why anyone would name a goat Tiger is beyond me, one of the children named her and it stuck. One of the boy goats was an ashy gray, with what seemed like, earrings on the side of his ears. Some goats have that; I thought it was so cute. His name was Charlie. His friend Milo was a handsome brown boy with black streak going down his head and through his back and tail. His handsomeness was only surpassed by his wit. I swear, I think he understood what I said and sometimes, even what I didn't say. So here I was expecting our first baby. They were all pregnant but Tiger was the first to go. I had bought a veterinary book that was very insightful and had devoured it, trying to learn as much as I could about the care of goats, especially now at this crucial time. But to read about it, is nothing like the actual thing, especially when you have never seen it before. The book said "the first thing you will

usually see is a dark, round bulge, the amniotic sac or water sac. This is closely followed by two feet and a tiny nose". She started passing stringy fluid tinged with blood and then a brown bulge like the book had said except there were no little feet or nose. She struggled to pass the brown bulge and started eating it; I was not sure what to do. She then laid down again and started pushing and this time I did see the little feet finally! And the little nose followed. She pushed and pushed and I grabbed hold of the little legs to help her when she pushed and it was out, but it was quiet and still, I held it upside down trying to get any fluid that might have remained in her lungs. She was beautiful and tiny; an ashy golden brown with a little white patch on her side, but I could not get her to breathe. I even tried giving mouth to mouth to her but nothing. She moved weakly and cried softly once and then nothing Tiger kept on licking her, staring at her, hoping for a miracle like I was, I think. My heart ached for this new mom and I cried with her for her labor and pain had only given birth to sorrow. I had to bury the tiny Molly, I thought she should have a name even though she never saw the light of day, or played with her cousins that were soon to come. Her mom had waited for her and so had I, and even for the briefest of time, she was here and I had loved and cried for her. It was hard to bury her on the frozen ground for it was on a winter's night that she had come and gone. Tiger called her for a week or so. I would see her looking for her, and then at me, asking me where I had taken her, and calling for her. Now, I know what happened. After seeing so many being born in all kinds of predicaments and after having been with the vet, the many times I had to call him to help me with a mom that's taking too long to deliver because she has tangled twins or a breached birth, or a baby that's too big for a first time mom. Tiger had Placenta Previa. That brown bulge I saw was not the amniotic sac but the placenta, that is why she ate it, but Molly was still inside. She suffocated without the oxygen provided by the placenta before she was able to breathe on her own. Millie had her baby a couple of weeks after. A little brown girl, she was named Matilda, we called her Tilly for short. Many soon followed.

The next residents to be brought to the farm were the sheep, four moms and twelve little ones. These were followed by two hundred chicks. We built an incubator with heat lamps to keep them warm. I had to raise them, for we had to have fresh eggs at the farm, or it could not be called a farm. Then a pony that was given to us, followed by a miniature donkey we purchase to be a guard animal. A white rabbit with black patches around the eyes came next, Bandit we called him. I don't think he knew what he was. He sometimes slept with the goats other times

with the sheep or donkey. With every new addition I would purchase abook on the care and needs of that particular animal. My favorite store then was tractor supply, where I could find anything I needed for my growing family.

You win some and lose some

*W*hile my family of animals was growing, my human family, however, seemed to be shrinking. We had moved to the farm when a friend of mine had asked me if I knew of a couple who could be interested in caring for a property that their employers had purchased in south Carolina, just an hour south of where we lived in Charlotte North Carolina. I immediately answered that I was interested. Of course they were looking for a couple, not a family. My husband was a maintenance technician at an apartment complex, where he was unhappy for some reason or other; this was his third job in a year. When he came home that afternoon I told him excitedly about the opportunity and how I thought it might be the answer to our prayers, that perhaps a change would be good for us. Besides his unhappiness with his job, we were having a hard time economically, making ends meet. Every month we would have to use a credit card for this or that because we would run out of money. Every month I would see the credit card bill getting higher and higher and I would stress over it. There were many nights I could not sleep thinking how we would get out of the hole that only seemed to get deeper and deeper with every year. Living with debt like this was new to me, I had been a single mother and even though I lived very simply with a small income, I had managed to purchase a small house for me and my kids and did not carry debt from one year to the next. My system had been to do with what I had, we always had fun, and I made sure of that. We would go out to dinner and outings with the kids and if I used credit, at the end of the year I made sure to pay it off with my tax return and go on a vacation with what was left. I start the year fresh with no debt.

We had been married four years when this opportunity came up, and we were deep in debt. I had asked him if he had any debts before we married, thinking I was covering all my bases, he answered that not really. As it turned out however, yes really he had. We spent the first two years of marriage paying off the debts he already had and acquiring new ones for he believed that if he wanted something he should not have to wait for it, he deserved it, he work hard and he had good credit, or rather I had good credit and we should use mine since it was better than his.

And if this was not enough to make anyone run for the hills, add a teenage daughter who hates the country, hates the step-dad, is constantly fighting with her brother because he took this or ate that of hers and you have home sweet home and marital bliss!.

My daughter was my first child; I had her when I myself was a child of eighteen. I am sure I was not a great mother to her, how could I be, a child myself, but I did the best I could for her. She always seemed in a hurry to grow up, precocious, hard headed, had to have her way and did not take well to being told what to do, so naturally she was the first to go. She had gotten a part time job and was going to college in charlotte; the commute was hard on her, so she moved in with my mother in charlotte. It was hard to see her go but I knew we all need to move on. I also knew that without me nagging her, she would get herself in more scrapes. And naturally, she had her share. She loved a good time and like most young folk, she never thought anything bad would happen to her, even if she made stupid choices and used poor judgment, but we must reap what we sow, it's unavoidable, sooner or later. She got a DUI and had her license suspended, and she spent a night in jail. She knew not to call me, I would not bail her out if I knew she was in the wrong and of course she was, there is no excuse for driving under the influence. I had often felt that my family was like a quilt, made up of different pieces all patched together, and I was very proud of it. Despite the problems we had, I would sometimes compare them to other families, and thought our issues were trivial compared to theirs. I felt happy, confident that we could make it through.

It came as a surprise to me, when one night, my husband announced he was leaving, citing he was not happy with his job, and country life and that he missed his friends in the city, that this was not a life for him. I tried to convince him that this was not the way to do things that we had to plan things. We had bills to pay.

"I see You!

When you laugh, I sing
When you sing, I dance
When you dream, I fly
When you cry, I hear you
When you stumble, I fall
When you fall, I bleed

When you are not looking
I see you!
You are a mother's hope.
Two stitches side by side
In a picture revealed by time
If you are pulled,
I become undone!
You are to me like no other
Was it not I
Who felt your first flutter?
You are your mother's daughter!
I want never to be apart
You have best quality heart!
I see you, I see you!

Sonia Lopez

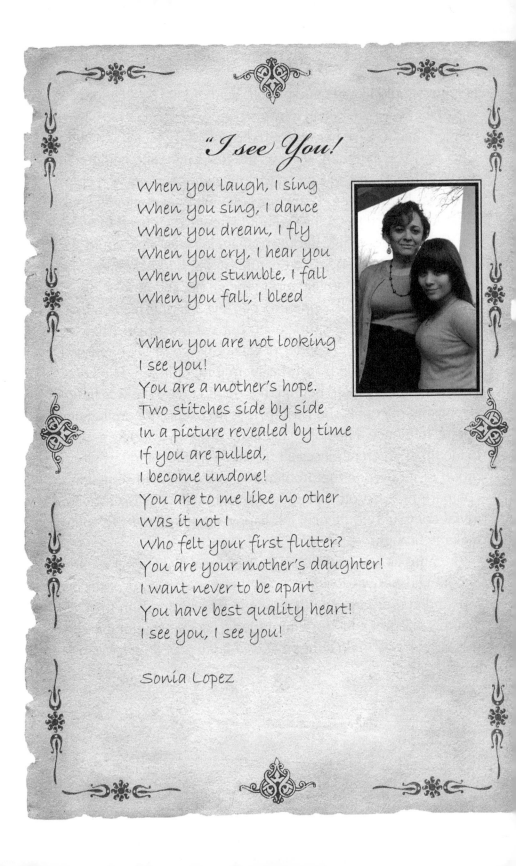

My son was close to the end of the school year and our employers were out of the country for another month. We needed to give enough notice. And what about where we would go; our house was leased for the next year. He said I could do whatever I wanted, those were my issues. He had to start his new job. He would be staying with a friend. My employers were in England at the time of this announcement. I could not up and leave, this was not just any job, where you can just up and leave. With my employers out of the country and the animals depending on me, I knew I had to remain. I wanted my son to finish the school year at least. He was not going to be happy when he found out he had to move schools again. It had been hard for him, coming from a big city to a country school where all the children were either White or Black. There were only maybe two other Spanish children in the school, so my son felt that the other children discriminated him for being different. He would tell me, "they call me Mexican" and "Go home Mexican" he would say "I told them I'm from Boston and that I am not Mexican, that I have never even been to Mexico but they keep calling me names". After a year there though, he had made friends, and the other kids started seeing him for who he was and I was sure he would not want to move. He did not do well with change. I kept repeating all this to myself through the night along with other questions. What was I going to do? Where would I go? My house was leased for the rest of the year. What would my family say? Was this another divorce in the horizon? I had to wait for my employers to return the following month, what would they say? Would they let me stay on? Should I start looking for another job? The pieces were becoming undone at the seams and I felt powerless to stop it.

A Time to Heal

*W*hen they returned, I was beyond embarrassed; I felt humiliated. I had to explain that my husband had left both me and the job without notice; that I understood if they most likely wanted to find a replacement and that I was willing to stay until they did. They were gracious and kind, however, and offered for me to stay and hire someone else to help. I could not believe it; I was so relieved to know I had time to figure out what I was going to do, and what had happened.

I spent many days in a daze, going about my chores as if on auto pilot. The days turned into weeks and the weeks into months, the months to years. I would spend a lot of time watching the animals, the simplicity of their lives. I would often wonder why our lives could not be so. Having been able to spend all that time outside in nature, sharing life with the animals, welcoming the little ones in Spring gave me so much joy. I was enjoying a peace I had not known in a long time.

It was not all fun and games by any means, it's a lot of work. My hands would freeze in the winter when the water for the animals froze and I had to break the surface of it so they could drink, Or when I would carry water from the house to give to three hundred plus chickens because the pipes froze. Cleaning the goat and sheep pens was a task that not many would find pleasant, both by the aromas and the back breaking job that shoveling load after load of s**t could be. But having all this time alone with my thoughts gave me, the so much needed time, I needed to heal. Both new wounds and old ones, that had been long neglected and ignored. I often felt like I had been running from one dog fight to the next, with no time to lick my wounds, no place to go and hide. I finally found a resting place, a quiet place, and time, time to think and be with myself. Time to find myself, in the maze that life seemed to be, with so many turns. Never knowing what you will find around the next corner or which is the best way to go.

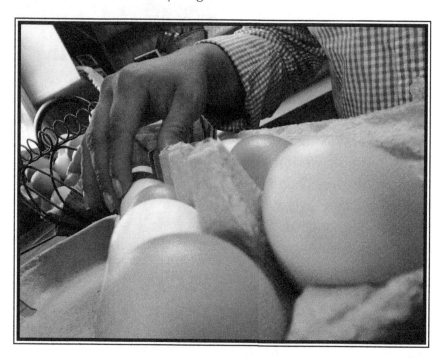

The Farm Tours

*M*any would come to visit the farm. Friends, family, and friends of my employer would come to see the growing farm. I had given so many tours I could tell every animal story in my sleep. The story of our first goats and how we lost them on their first week here. They ran away, they were looking for their original home. We found them a week later about a mile away. My pony, Lupita, she had a little girl as her original owner but with the economy they could no longer keep her. She had been given to some neighbors of ours who had teenage sons. Them along with their friends would chase her and ride her and ended up traumatizing her to the point that she runs away as soon as she sees boys or strange men around. She is a beautiful pony, rusty red with white socks and a white mark on her forehead and a long blond mane she loves to be brushed and apples as a treat.

Answering questions about eggs was a large part of the tour. Especially when children were part of the group. I would give them their own basket and ask them if they would like to help me collect the eggs. As we went along I would explain that not all the eggs under the hen were laid by her, only one. The others were laid by her friends but they all like particular nests and take turns laying eggs in the same one. No, these eggs will not hatch into little chicks because there is no rooster in the coop; the rooster is the daddy chicken. If there was a daddy chicken it would take 21 days for the eggs to hatch if the mom sat on them and kept them warm. Eggs can be kept unrefrigerated up to three weeks and up to six weeks refrigerated. If you don't know how old an egg is and you want to know if it is still good, place it in bowl filled with water, if it is still good it will sink to the bottom. If it floats, do not eat it! We had different kinds of hens and they all lay different kind of eggs. We had Rhode Island reds; they lay brown eggs. The white ones are called White Leghorn, and they lay white eggs. And the speckled brown ones are called Uracanas and they lay the blue and green eggs. Nutritionally they are all the same.

The goats love it when children came to farm too, they knew

they would get extra treats from the kids; they would come running when I would call them. "Come on girls, come say hello to the children". They would stand on their back legs and fight for attention and for the bread or crackers that was given out. I introduce everyone to the goats and hand little pails filled with sweet feed, the goats smell it and put on a show for the kids, they will do anything for the molasses and grain in those pails. Sylvia is large dairy goat given to us by a neighbor that could no longer keep her. Somehow she always found a way into their shed where the feed was kept and made a mess of it. She likes to follow me around. She thinks she is human. She likes having afternoon tea with me and lies outside the front door waiting for me hoping she will get a cookie, she loves sweets. She is a great

girl though pesky at times. If it was not for her, many of my orphaned sheep would not have made it. She could produce half a gallon of milk, if not more. She would stay still if I gave her enough treats so I could milk her.

It amazes me now how we enclose ourselves from the natural world. Not long ago I was also afraid of the animals, asked if the sheep bite like the guest were asking now. My son Mickey was even afraid to go outside because of the bees and other bugs. We had to relearn to live in this wonderful world we isolate ourselves from. We spend our time inside our homes or buildings with air conditioning, and from there to our cars. We forget how good a morning walk in the crisp morning air can be, or during a hot summer day, after a hard day's work, to have a cool afternoon breeze whisper in your ear. I learned to listen again. You can hear so much more in the silence of the country than in clutter of noise we live in the city. The television, the radio, the computer, the phone, they block all the real sounds until we become deaf. The symphony of birds singing in the morning goes unheard. The concert put on by the crickets and the frogs in the afternoon is lost. The sun goes out of his way each day to paint the sky with reds, purples, orange and gold. Before he goes to bed he puts it all on display, only a few will take their eyes away from their screens to look up. He is not discouraged by this, in the morning he will put on a show again, only to be missed. His spotlight taken over by the red of taillights and the hurried glances to the clock. We don't spend enough time outside. We cover our feet with shoes and we put cement down so we never have contact with the ground. All our food comes from the ground but we don't want to put our hands in it, to till it, to reap our food from it. Maybe we are afraid because we know that that is where we will end up. We have become not only deaf but nearsighted. We only see what is directly in front of us, and have forgotten to look down at the ground that feeds us and the sky that sustains us.

Many times I had to come to the stables at night to check on a sheep that was expecting to give birth, with only the moon for light. I would stare at the heavens and marvel at the amazing display of stars in the firmament. When I looked up, my problems seemed so small. I imagine myself out there looking down and the earth, a small speck, among the giants that were the stars and galaxies, I imagine myself in that small speck, even smaller. Did it matter, all this that seemed to consume us? I won' t deny that at times I felt like a loser, lonely, and afraid, but being surrounded by the animals and the beauty of the land helped me put it all on the back burner. Working at this farm was helping me see what I had and not what I had lost. I was seeing everything in a new light. I felt like a tree in the fall when the cold winds have scattered its leaves and faces the winter, alone and cold but with a hope of a Spring to come.

The fall

I once stood tall
Full of promise, green!
My arms were strong and full
With lovers at play and song.

The warmth has gone
Chased by autumn's wind
And in its place has left
A lonely chill and an empty nest

Summer's passions painted me crimson red
With dreams and hopes of gold..
One by one they fall and fall
At my feet they gather and make their bed

Now alone, I am bent
With my face to the wind
And what's left at my feet
The pain is so great, I pray for winter's sleep

Where I can dream my dreams
And fly free from old man's frigid grip
I will gather strength from what is left behind
Up my roots will come, and fill my arms again

When my loves come back to me
Springing forth a song
And the warmth of a sweet embrace
And for this, I wait....

Sonia Lopez

At Another Farm in Another Time

*W*hile giving a tour one day, one of the children was walking with me and asked me why I lived here at the farm. The question by this child started me in a journey. This was not the first farm I had been on, though it seemed like it from my having to learn everything. It had been long ago, it almost seemed to have been another lifetime.

I embarked in search of lost and forgotten memories buried deep. They heard me calling for them. Memories started moving, coming out of the shadows where they had been banished. Slowly and shyly at first, as if afraid they might be sent back any minute. But then they started rushing in, crowding all around me, and speaking all at once. I started getting to know them all over again one by one. They had all been there waiting for me to come back for them, afraid they had been forgotten forever.

I remember lying on his chest on a hammock, the sway of it combined with his scent, how secure I felt. I remember how I would wait for him to come home. We lived atop of a hill and I would strain to hear his truck coming. I could hear it way before I could see it and I would run down the hill to meet him, my brothers and sisters running with me. After everyone had calmed down, he would find me without anyone else seeing, he would give me a piece of candy he had been hiding for me. How special I felt.

My father had been a farmer all his life. He grew corn, rice and beans. He also raised dairy cows and at my house there was always an array of animals that were part of the family. I remember at planting season, how he would bind the steer to the yoke. He handed me a little pouch with pink corn seeds in it. He walked behind the steer guiding the plow tilling the ground. I would follow behind him. I would drop my seeds and with my feet I would cover them with the newly moved earth. As I went along I search for colored pieces of glass that would surface as we went along. All the while I listened to him saying how

he hoped for rain to make the grains we had just dropped become a cornfield. I can still smell the freshly tilled earth when the rains started coming down. All my early memories are of a happy time in a farm, working with my father and playing with my brothers and sisters. There was a tall tree in front of our house at the bottom of the hill and in the afternoon it would fill up with birds whose tails resembled scissors, hundreds of them, making the most amazing noise. We would sit there on the red clay at the top the hill and stare at them as they would take off in masses and do their dance in the sky for us to see. When they returned to the tree another group would go up and perform their dance. I would sit there mesmerized at the display. Those happy memories came to an end. A storm of turmoil was brewing both in my home and in my country. Communism was trying to make a home in my world and the guerrillas were making their way to villages like mine, bringing with them destruction and the most unspeakable atrocities you can imagine. It was around this time my parents separated. My mother left with Lore, one of my sisters and left my father with the remaining seven. Gris was the oldest girl, thirteen. My oldest brother must have been fifteen, I thought he was all grown at the time but he was just a boy. My father would send him to another part of the country in the coast to care for the cattle he had there and we would not see him for months. When he came, he would always bring all kinds of things for us, fruits, vegetables and dried fish that he had caught himself along with shrimp. I loved to hear his stories of his life in the coast with the cattle.

My mother had a sister in the United States and moved there with my sister. I would not see her for five years. In the meantime our home was chaos. My father would drink a lot and my sister did not know how to cook or take care of the house. We were like wild children. I had a great imagination for company though, and I could imagine that it was all a great adventure. I would climb the Papaya trees in our yard or Mangoes if I was hungry. An aunt of mine had these tiny bananas that look like fat fingers in her orchard, I would go there and borrow some when I got tired of my papayas, if her dog did not hear me. He was a mean one. I put rocks in my pockets just in case. My wild days were numbered though; my father soon found himself a woman and brought her home. I don't know how my father convinced her to come to a house full of wild children but I guess the fact that she was expecting one as well helped her make up her mind. I really wanted her to like me and tried hard to do as she said. We started becoming second class citizens in our own home when she started having children. Of course I would have an opinion that I would voice, that did not help me in my campaign to gain her approval. There were three born while I was there. I would see how they had new clothes while my two younger brothers ran around naked because they had none. We were soon sent to the city, to go to school, or to get us out of my stepmoms hair. My oldest brother had left and joined my mother a year or two after she left. He started working to help my mother bring us to join them too. Gris was next to leave, I had never been separated from her and I hated to see her go. Soon after, in a few months' time, another ticket was sent for my brother Romeo. He did not want to go, however, and I took his place. I was eleven at the time. I remember spending the day with my father. He bought me two outfits I would wear on my trip and he took me to a foreign exchange to buy some dollars for me to take with me. He brought me to a bus station where I joined a lady that was taking me to my mother in the United States. He handed me all the money he had made that day. I saw the tears in his eyes. He must have known that he would not see me again. This farmer was the most important person in my life up to this point and I was saying good bye and when I turned away from him I never turned back. I faced my new life in a different land and I never wrote or called and I forgot…

It saddens me that I never got to tell him how much he had meant to me. He probably thought we all forgot him and he never knew how much his love shaped the person I became. I saw him one last time a few years back, but he did not see me. I saw him through the glass of his casket. He had arranged his own funeral. He had even arranged for a band to play music from the house where the wake took place all the way to the cemetery. We had to walk next to the car that carried the casket under the blistering sun in San Vicente, all of us, the children from his first wife.

At first none of us thought we would go. I was working as a nursing assistant in a nursing home in Charlotte when I got the call. I did not know what to make of it. Before my shift ended though I knew I was going to go back to that place where I had been so happy, I needed to say goodbye even if he was not there to say it back. Before the day was done I had spoken to all my brothers and sisters and one by one they had all arranged to go as well. I was happy and relieved to know we were all going. A cousin of us let us borrow his house in San Vicente. I was so happy we were going to be all together in the same place after a long time.

They had found his body hanging from a beam in his house with a letter, leaving his house and land to my youngest brothers. We went to the house the day after the funeral. I could not help looking up at the beam where his body was found. I kept trying to imagine what his last thoughts had been. He had been all alone the last years of his life. Regrets and sorrows were probably all he had for company. My mother had left him, then one by one we had left. My stepmom had five children with my father and they had all gone too. He had watched everyone leave.

The police report said that there was evidence that he had not been alone that day; there were alcohol bottles and Diazepam pills in the house as if someone had been drinking with him. There was the suspicion that he might have been killed and the suicide letter planted but the case went cold and eventually closed. I guess we will never know for sure what really happened. For a time I thought that the man that killed my sister had killed him, he had vowed to do it. After he killed my sister he had ran back to El Salvador and my father had found out where he was staying, got the police to come with him and waited for him. He knew what bus he would take and the time;

he had many friends that informed him of his whereabouts. So he waited for him with the police and they captured him. My sister's murderer was captured and sentenced to serve twenty years in one of the worst prisons in El Salvador. He got out after serving ten for good behavior so it is possible that he did it, he had enough motives and he had killed many before. After my sister was killed people started talking about how he had served in the Guardia Nacional and had killed many before, Information that came a little too late. And perhaps it would not have mattered anyhow; my sister was one of those women that thought people could change and that everyone deserves a chance. She thought there was good in everyone so I don't know if it would have made any difference. She was gone and now my dad was gone too. My Father arranged to be buried with her in the family crypt. I watched as two men sealed it with cement and bricks after his casket was placed inside.

We had all come together this last time to say good bye, and he never knew that we had all been there, regretting not having said good bye.

I return from my journey in time and realize why this farm has such a pull on me; it's the little girl in me that was taken away from her home, her dad and her land. In this farm I found a piece of me that was lost.

He taught me to love the land and the animals. When I am with them, he is there. When I plant my seeds, he is still ahead of me telling me how. When you see me barefoot in the field talking to the goats, it's not me, it's a little girl they used to call Lupita, corriendo sin zapatos detras de su Papi, su heroe, su primer amor.

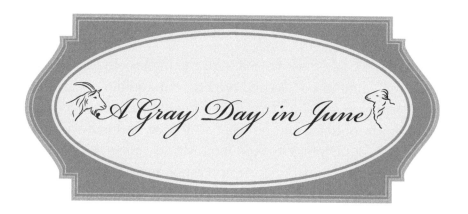

A Gray Day in June

ummer is here and is a hot one! The secret to farming in the summer is getting up early and doing all the outdoor chores before the heat makes it unbearable. It is June; two more months of this. I start by feeding the goats a small amount of all stock sweet feed in the morning. They love this stuff and fight for it. I set it out in different feeders to make sure everyone gets their share. Lupita, my pony gets her share too. I love to rub her down when she is eating. Then I go see Chester. He is a miniature donkey. We got him to be a guard animal for the sheep. We use to get a lot of coyotes in this area, not so much last year. Anyway Mr. Chester turned out to be not such a good guard animal. He attacked two of my lambs. I was able to save one, the other one died as a result of the attack. He would bite them by the back of the neck and swing them around and not let go until I took them from him. My heart ached when

I saw the bloody mess he made of my babies. The first time I found the lamb bloodied and bruised and could not figure out what had happened until I caught him in the act. I had to separate him from them and he has had to live on his own until I can figure out what to do with him. My vet thinks it is because he has not been castrated yet, too much testosterone. You see he is in love with my Lupita but she is too tall for him and he gets frustrated chasing her all day. He took out his frustration on my innocent babies. I have told him I am going to build him a ramp so he can reach her and they can make a beautiful mule together. I probably should not give him false hope but I feel so bad for him. Its agony to love and see the object of your affection go galloping by and know that it will never be; so close and yet so far. Now I head out to the sheep. They are penned up and I won't let them out until I set out the food for them, otherwise, they would trample me trying to get it. They all come at me at the same time and push me and with their heads in the way I can't scoop the feed into the feeders. I have three long wooden feeders, where I set out the food for them. I see them looking at me, waiting by the gate. They all want to be first. I head to the gate and open it, and it's a stampede to get to the food. The little ones stay behind out of the way. They are happy to play with each other. While they enjoy their breakfast, I brush the water containers with a little bleach, is the only thing that keeps this green stuff from growing in this heat. I will have to come back and refill the water later. They drink so much in the summer and the water gets too hot at midday. The chicken coop is my last stop. They are all waiting for me too. They know the routine. We have them separated according to age into three areas so I bring a bucket of feed to all the feeders and fill them up. I love to watch them as they search out for the seeds they like. I premix the layers feed mash along with scratch grains. I let them out by

turns into the fields so they can have grass. They love to go out exploring looking for worms and scratching the ground. I find the holes later where they had their dust baths. We built them a small door we open so they can go out. We tried leaving the regular door opened and found the sheep in the coop eating the chicken feed so we came up with a door just big enough to let a chicken out. You see them lining up to go out. In the afternoon when the sun starts to go down you see them looking for the door to come back in. I come and check to make sure everyone got back and close the door so predators don't get in.

As I get ready to head back to the house I notice one of the ewes separate herself from the herd going into the field. She is pregnant. She was one of the first to give birth in December and somehow must have gotten pregnant right away in one of those times the male got out of his pen to enjoy the company of the ladies. I don't like them having more than one birth a year, it doesn't give them enough time to recover. She is one of the first ones we purchased. We originally got twelve lambs and four grown moms. I remember she was pregnant when we got her, had her babies in July that time. She is huge; she must have twins if not more. I am going to have to pen her up so I can keep an eye on her. I close the gate that leads to the fields after all the others leave and then I get a pail with the sweet feed so she will follow me into the pens I have ready in the stable. I have found that the best thing is to give them a safe, clean, quiet place so they can do their thing. The least you intervene the better. They are very nervous creatures, so I don't like to give them any added stress. Once they start it's quick, but every once in a while you have trouble. If I see that she starts labor and does not progress, it is usually that the babies are not in the right position. I have plastic gloves that go past my elbows, and lubricant. There have been occasions where I have had to go in and get them situated so they can come out. Their two front feet have to come out first with their little hoofs pointing up. Sometimes one leg is bent backwards or both and the mom can't get the shoulders out that way. I will give her an hour and come back to check on her. I walk back to the house and set a pot of coffee on, I think I will make myself a couple of eggs over easy should do it with some toasted tortillas. It's been a couple of years since my husband left and I spend a lot of time in this kitchen talking to myself. My son is in school all day and there are days I don't see anyone at all so I have learned to enjoy my own company. When he first left I had a hard time doing things by myself. I could not go to a restaurant or a movie, it felt odd, it was not that I missed him, more like you are so used to being with someone that when, you are first alone, you don't know what to do. It took me a long time for example, to use up all the bed. I would stay on my side and not mess up his side, until one day I made myself sprawl all over it, telling myself, "this is all my bed, he is not coming back". Anything I was afraid to do or felt uncomfortable doing something, I would do it just to get over it. The first time I went to a restaurant by myself (because I was really craving a steak) I sat at the bar so I would not feel so odd. I would watch the game, ordered a beer and enjoy my steak, it was so liberating. Before this I used to feel like people would be looking at me and feel sorry for me and think, "oh poor lady, she can't get a date and has to eat by herself". After a while, I did not care what people said or thought, if they looked my way I would just smile and that was the end of it. A piece of steak would have been great with these eggs by the way. I got to go and see how my girl is doing; most likely she will have had her babies already. Let me get some iodine and my scissors so I can cut the umbilical cords. The moms bite it but sometimes, it is still too long, and it drags on the floor or the babies step on it

and they can get infected so I like to cut them short, an inch and a half to two inches then I dip the cord in iodine. I use a shot glass filled with the Iodine, I hold it against their bellies and let the tip soak in it for a bit. I look in the stable but she is panting and nothing. With this heat she is going to get really tired. I put my gloves on but I can't find any little legs and the mom is not letting me do more. I am going to have to call the vet. He is a country vet and does house calls to the neighboring farms. He does mainly large animals like horses and cattle and has come out to help me out when I have not been able to help them on my own. He is very helpful and answers my questions. He comes an hour later, after checking her he tells me that one of the babies is laying right across the cervix and that that is why she is not progressing. He goes in and after a lot of maneuvering he pushes him in the right direction, gets hold of the legs and pulls the first one out. They come out covered in slime, very slippery. He goes back in and takes out the second one. The mom immediately starts licking them clean and they start trying to stand and look for her teats. The vet goes out of the stall to wash his hands and change his gloves and tells me to check to make sure we got them all, and to my surprise there is another set of legs in there. I gently help him out. He is small, but shaking the slime out of his mouth and nose a good sign. Now I only have to wait for the placentas. He gives her a couple of shots. One for infection and another to help her expel the placentas.

The next day she was not better. She would not get up and I knew she was not going to make it. Her whole uterus came out and she bled out. Here I was with three orphaned lambs. My son was away in Boston for vacation. How was I going to get her up and dispose of her body? I had no one to help me at the farm at the time. I called a boy, a school mate of my son from a neighboring farm and he came to help me. We grabbed her by the legs and picked her up on a wheel barrel and decided that the best thing was to burn the remains. She must have weighed one hundred twenty pounds. There was no way I could dig a hole that big, and with this heat, I was afraid of the smell and wild animals digging her up. So we took her at the very back of the property. We got a good fire going and then put her on top of it and added more wood. I hated to see her burning and the smell of shared wool and skin. I hated even more, thinking about those babies that would grow up without their mother. I hate the feeling of hopelessness, anger; despair that comes with death… death had visited me too, on a hot day in June twenty-three years ago.

June 6, 1988
Un Dia Gris

*I*t is so hot! The waves hit the barge; I am laying face down looking down into the water of the Charles River. I have never seen so many jelly fish. They are floating, bobbing up and down. The waves lull me. I wish I could go to sleep here and now. I wish I could go to sleep and never wake up. I have been up now for more than twenty-four hours. The Tobin Bridge is above me. I hear the horns and engines but they seemed so far, like in a dream. Life goes on as if nothing. How can they go on as if nothing? How can I go on? I keep playing the scene in my head and think it can't be; it has to be a mistake. Just yesterday morning she asked me if I wanted to finish her breakfast. She was leaving for school. She was late. She would graduate at the end of June as a medical assistant. I had finished her breakfast; huevos revueltos con frijoles fritos, crema y tortillas tostadas. She had left.. She said bye Lupi, those were her last words to me but I can't remember her voice anymore. I hate not being able to remember her voice! I walked to school that day. I was sixteen that year and in the tenth grade at Chelsea High, in the old buildings not the new school. I don't remember much of the day, just coming home to lots of people and police cars. That was not uncommon on Essex St. in Chelsea those days, so I was not alarmed. I went up the steps to my house, we lived on the second floor, and the house had a porch on the first floor. There was someone there and I asked "did they find out about my drug operation?" a man I knew answered, "Julio killed your sister" he said this as if he was commenting on the weather. I shouted back at him, "Don't joke like that stupid!" and I ran upstairs. There were people here too, surrounding Mami and she is crying and she won't stop. No, no it cannot be true! It has to be a mistake! I just saw her! It must have been somebody else! Then it's just a blur of noise and images, people coming and going and the tears that blind and sting. The pain in the chest, the helplessness, I cry and cry until I think I can't cry anymore, until a new wave of tears come and I welcome them, because I never want to feel joy again, not if she won't be here to share it. I go into my room to try to get away from all these people; I wish they would all just go away. It's not just my room, but our room. We have shared a room ever since I can remember, first with others in the family but for the past couple of years it has just been the two of us. Our "we are the world" poster is on the wall. Our chucks lay scattered on the floor along with discarded clothes from this morning. She bought them for us, hers are peach and mine pink. We spent many nights here talking before going to sleep. We listen to David Allan Bushey's bedtime magic on the radio. We would leave it on all night with the volume low. "Lean on me" was one of her favorite songs that summer. That was my sister Daisy, When we were little we called her Gris, short for Griselda, her middle name. We all changed from using our middle names to our first when we came to the States. Her nickname suited her though, Gris, like a gray, rainy day for she always seemed sad, like her heart was away somewhere. Sometimes I think she worried about the rest of my brothers that had been left behind and somehow still felt responsible for them. She worked and went to school and always saved to send money to them back home. The three youngest still remained in El Salvador, my home country. They probably would not remember much of their oldest sister that had tried to be a mother to all of them, a load much too big, for a scared thirteen year old girl that needed a mom too. I wish they had known her. They were nine, seven and six when she left. What they probably remember most is going to the airport to receive the casket of their sister who had left to the United States to escape the violence of war, only to find it next door. Her fiancée lived on the house next to us. They had been dating for about a year. He was my mother's favorite son in law. He would bring her flowers on mother's day and would take her on her errands. My sister had tried to break up with him a couple of times. She never told me why but he always convinced her to continue the engagement. He would cry and bring her all kinds of gifts to make up with her. Maybe he had been violent to her and she was afraid to tell. The night before he killed her, the wind was howling outside, and she told me she wanted to end it, that she did not want to marry him. I told her "don't marry him then, you don't have to marry him if you don't want to". That morning I heard her call him, he would drive her to school and I heard him say to stop by that he was having coffee. She must have gone in and maybe she tried to tell him that she did not want to marry him anymore and he killed her. She left the house at seven-thirty and the coroner placed time of death a nine. There were other people in the house but no one said anything or went next door to tell my mother until one in the afternoon, enough time for him to drive out of the state. Someone came and got my brother Romeo, seventeen at the time, to come to see his sister. He was the first on the scene. I cannot imagine the horror it must have been for him to see his sister all cut up, he had stabbed her many times and there was blood everywhere. Her hand prints were on the wall and on the telephone lines, as if she had tried to get help. She was twenty-three when she died, and she has been gone twenty-three years this June. So now she has been gone for as long as she was here. I have missed her every day since. She was not just my sister; she was a mom and a friend. Until she comes back, a part of me will always be Gris.

Daisy with Cousin Toni

John 5:28, 29

The Family

*T*he sun has stretched his arms. With a yawn, he looks around a final time. He bathes the fields with a warm orange glow. He has said "enough for one day, it's time for bed". Its late September, when cooler temps descend at night, but in the afternoons we are often blessed with warmth. I have come to check on my girls, my goats. I like to sit and watch them wind down from the day and look for their spot for the night. The little ones refuse to let this day be done. They are still chasing each other. Jumping unto the rocks and ramps we build for them and then off again. They show off even more if they know they are being watched. They will settle after a while and start looking for their moms and the spot they chose for them. They will all lie together for the night, the family. My Tiger has a big family now. The year following Molly's loss she had twins, one boy and a girl. We did not keep him too long. Boys are extremely cute when they are babies but as adolescents, they are terrible. They chase the girls all day long, they pee on their face, supposedly makes them more attractive to them. If you have ever had a billy goat you know where the expression "randy as a goat" comes from. So we don't keep the boys too long. And we don't want them interbreeding so we usually sell them when my employer is away somewhere because she doesn't like to see any of them

go. We keep the girls though, I named Tiger's daughter, Punky, and she had another set of twins after that. Punky is also a mom. At night they gather in groups, the ones that have had daughters have the bigger families. This year are Tiger and her twins and Punky with her little boy lying together. Millie has a baby girl this year, twin girls from last year Nayi and Daly and Matilda, our first baby goat that we had at the farm. She has had two girls one last year and another this year, and they are all together. Diana had a boy the first year, so he is not here anymore but last year she had a girl. And she has had twin boys this year. Both Diana and her daughter are completely black, her twins this year are both blonde. I had been waiting for her to have her babies. She was the last to deliver this year. I had been around all morning, I had a feeling she would start any minute. I had gone to do something or other and when I returned, I did not see her and I knew she had delivered them without me. I went into the stall and she looked so proud of herself as if saying "look at my boys, aren't they beautiful?" and they were!. I told her what a good job she did and how proud I was of her. Her daughter had a girl. One of the children that came to visit named her Kate. She was born with a birth defect. No acchiles tendon. She had to have the leg amputated so she would not drag the stump on the mud. We were afraid of infection. The fact that she only has three legs instead of four does not seem to slow her down though, she plays and chases the others and goes about her business as usual. You can't miss what you never had, I guess.

The human family is a place where one can find warmth, companionship, protection and comfort too. I feel blessed to have come from a large family. Even though, imperfect like all families, dysfunctional at times, I can say with all honesty, they did the best they could, with what they had. It is easy to judge your parents harshly. We might think that, the way they did things was barbaric. If we try to see them objectively though, and take into account their time and their own upbringing and the culture they grew up in. maybe then we would find it easier to be forgiving and see beyond it to the efforts they put forth to raise us the way they thought was best. Discipline for example; was from today's standards barbaric and cruel. In my father's time to get whipped with a piece of rope or belt was normal. That was how most parents punished a disobedient child. I'm sure he got quite a few of those when he was young. That was what he learnt parenting was, and that is how he punished us. The advantage of having a large family was that we always had someone to play with. We always had someone to talk to. We always had someone to fight with. We always had someone to cry with.

Family is where you came from, is what has shaped you. Family is what you bring to it. If you don't take it for granted it will always be there to help you pick up the pieces.

I would not change my family even if I could. If I did, I would no longer be me. Without me, would they be complete?

I wish I had known those that came before, our roots, the grandparents and the great grandparents. What their hopes were, what they dreamed about. I just had a glimpse of my grandfathers. I was not fortunate to meet my grandmothers. Their legacy was the example they gave, patience, humility, loyalty and forgiveness. I want to know the new ones coming and the ones still to come, the new leaves and branches. What can I leave behind for them? What lessons to pass on? Will I have a part in the shape they will have? We are all connected, the family, a circle. From the ground where our roots lay, our ancestors, to the trunk we are now, supporting the new growth. Hoping they will have a better season than the one we had.

The lessons learned…

That no matter how somber today might seem, there is always tomorrow.

That there is strength inside you.

That you can always stand up and try again.

That your past does not define you, learn from it and go on.

That only you can decide your worth.

When you hold back and just gather you end up with less but when you are generous and give to others you end up with more.

Things are just things, they can be replaced. Our most valuable possession is each other.

When we hold on to each other, we are strong.

When we learn from each other, we are wise

When we feed each other, we are full.

When you count your blessings you realize how fortunate you are and you are more grateful.

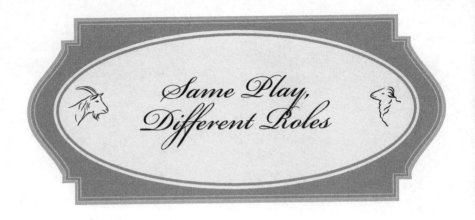

Same Play, Different Roles

*I*n life and in family you write your part and act it out as you go. I used to think that life just happened to you. Like a ship at sea without a captain at the mercy of the the wind, the currents and the storms that will inevitably come. The reality, nonetheless, is that a lot of what happens in our life can be altered by us, if we want to. We can choose to be the captain of our vessel, we can learn to sail. Let our masts be filled with dreams. Ride the currents and let them take us to ports of adventure. Face the storms or go around them. We decide what sort of person we want to be. We give shape to our character and decide how we are to play the roles we are given.

The variety of roles can make the voyage interesting. A daughter, a granddaughter, a sister, a mother, an aunt, and a friend. How we play our roles can deeply affect our fellow passengers for it's a game we are all playing at the same time.

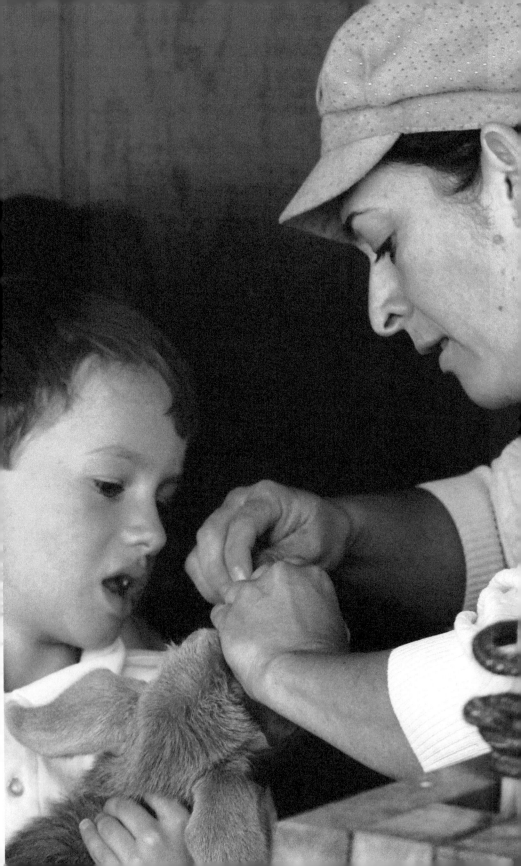

A Granddaughter

I was a granddaughter once. I loved my grandfather. He was my mother's father. I called him Papita. When he came to visit, I would sit on his lap. He had a polyester shirt that depicted elephants in a circus. I would stare at it for hours and imagine being part of a circus. He would tell me stories while he braided my hair. He would make ribbons out of corn husks to tie them. He brought oranges to us. He had a pocket knife that he would use to peel them for me. He would start at the top and go around until he reached the bottom without a break. I would play with the peels, I would squeeze the zest into a lighted candil, and I liked the blue light it created. He cut the orange in half and shakes a little salt on it for me or separates the segments for me to eat.

When my mother left I was afraid I would not see him anymore. My father had threatened him not to come around anymore. He was angry at my mother for leaving and took it out on him. He never stopped coming though. He would sneak in, even after father caught him once. My father came after him with a machete, we were all afraid he was going to kill him. My brother Vila was home that time and he put himself in front of the machete protecting grandfather and told my father, "you are going to have to kill me first dad" my grandfather ran off then.

I found the molasses at the bottom of the hill later that day that he had brought. It was frothy light brown; he would get it from a sugarcane processing. I stuck my fingers in it and lick them, so sweet! Even sweeter knowing he risked his life just to bring it to us, and knowing he loved us and would not abandon us. I always looked forward to his visits. He showed me what loyalty is. Sticking to those you love, no matter what. He did untill the end. He loved his girls, my mom and her sister, and their children. He lived for them, for me. When my turn came to be there for him, I tried hard to be there for him. I would visit regularly and listen to his stories. He loved telling stories of his youth and of relatives that are no longer alive. I would bring him oranges like he had brought me, and bananas. He loved cheese puffs, chicken, Coke and Ensure. I would call and ask what to bring even though I already knew the list, it was the same things he ask for. I would get him dressed and take him to the Kingdom hall meetings he enjoyed so much, even if he could hardly hear. I bought him a headphone set to help him hear better and he loved to go with me and sing Kingdom melodies.

He had a good run .He was ninety-six years old when he died. He enjoyed his life, had many friends, and traveled. He was grateful and forgiving. If I am ever a grandmother, I have his script. I hope I can play the part half as well as he did.

I got the call I had been waiting for, one night I was driving back to the farm. I felt sorry he had not seen the farm, he would have loved it. He had broken his hip a few years back and had never been the same. He walked with a walker and used a wheelchair but this last year he spent most in bed. The last time I visited him he told me " ya llego el paraiso nana, vi a la Ricarda" he was happy. And I had prayed for him to stop suffering. He had fallen many times. He would get confused and climb the furniture imagining who knows what and get hurt. He passed away one night, my sister Lore and my Mom had been with him. He died at home. We had him cremated. They gave me a little box with his ashes. I put the box of ashes in a gift bag and they have been with me for a year now in my living room. I can't seem to make myself plant him in the garden like I said I would. I know I am going to have to leave this place someday and I don't want to leave his ashes behind. I think he would want me to take them with me when I leave and plant him in my garden. Reminds me of the story of Joseph in the Bible when he tells the Israelites not to leave his bones behind when they leave Egypt to go to the Promised Land. I will leave him where he is for now, in the gift bag. That is what he was to me any-way… a gift from God.

A Sister

$\mathcal{I}$ feel sorry for those that have never had a sister. I was blessed with three, two older ones and one younger one. The oldest, Gris, took her job of big sister very seriously. I used to sleep with her when I was little; she was a second mom to me. My sister Lore was the older sister I wanted to be like. Always neat and sophisticated. I would be jealous of her because she was so pretty. She would wear her hair in curls like Shirley Temple in the movies. Mine was always a mess. I wanted to look pretty and stay clean, but it was so hard to do when I had to climb the trees and chase the boys with my sling shot to avenge my friends. She would wear her socks up to her knees, I wore scrapes and bruises and shoes made my feet hot, so mud suited me better. She was a tough act to follow. (I am still trying; I wear shoes most of the time now). When my turn came around to be a big sister, I loved it. My little sister Norma, she was mine. I did not have to fight for her, my older sisters must have been tired of taking care of babies and children. My mother never failed to bring a new one every year. I would show her things I had learned and convince to come along on my adventures. Sometimes we would just climb a mango tree in the back of the house and hide there, we would bring a salt shaker with us to eat the green mangoes till we were nauseous and talk about the stories we made up in our minds. We used to call our game "vamos a jugar diabla" it meant that we would talk, away from the rest, especially my stepmom we did not want her to hear our dreams, they were our escape from reality. She would make fun of us if she heard. People use to think we were twins. I am two years older but there was not much difference of height between us. They would make our dresses from the same material. I would hold her hand everywhere we went.

When I left to come to the States she was ten and I did not see her again until she was eighteen. The night she came we stayed up all night talking and it was as if we had never been apart, we picked up right where we had left. She did not even need to speak, for me to understand. It was as if I could hear her thoughts and she mine.

When I lost my sister Gris it made me realize how precious sisters were and I wanted to enjoy each day with them and have no regrets of not having said this or done that with them. I love having been blessed with sisters and I have loved being one.

My Spot

From my spot I looked up and there were two
And to my side, an inch or so below, was one
I hold her hand, we are dressed alike
We are like two peas in a pod

The first is too young and unprepared
For the load she has to bear
A whole brood not hers to care
She does without complaint and without
    despair
For one day soon, she will have three, taking
    care of her

The second is very neat!
With socks to her knees and perfect pleats
Mami's pride and joy, her head full of
    bouncy curls
Makes the boys skip a beat!

In my spot, my feet are bare
My face is smudged; there are knots in
    my hair!
Don't know what part is mine
Don't want my lot, don't like my spot!

The one, I left your hand, we were pulled apart
All alone you had to stand
To the wrong side you never strayed
And in my heart, your hand in mine
   always stayed

What did I ever do?
To have three like you!
Pearls in a sea of time
Strung together by waves of chance

I have the perfect spot
Where I can look up at two
And walk beside the one.

To my sisters with love.

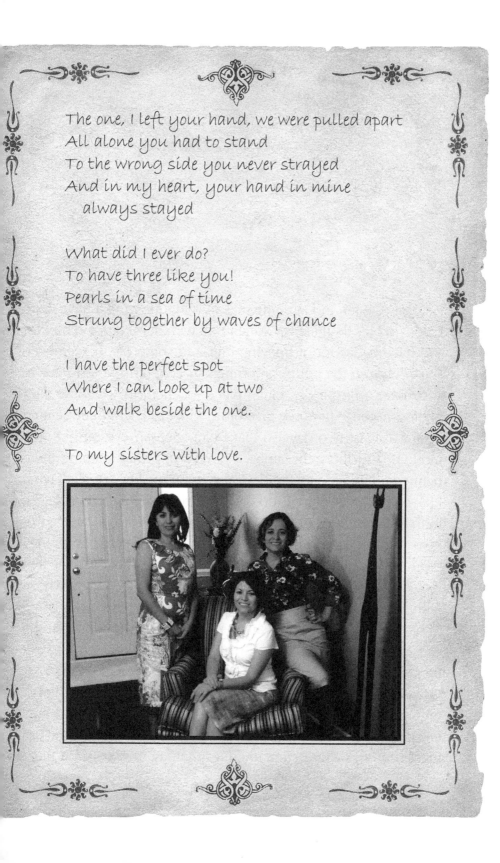

A Mother

*I*ts winter and lambing season is in full swing. I have more babies than I know what to do with. It is cold and muddy. We have had a lot of freezing rain and some ice. It seems the sheep choose the coldest mornings to give birth, and I have to scramble to find a dry, clean place for them to welcome their babies, home. After they give birth, I like to keep them penned up for at least two days so that I can keep an eye on both the mothers and the new lambs. I have found that keeping them penned up for a couple of days also helps me keep track of what I have. How many boys, how many girls and which moms gave birth to them. Most of the ewes have ear tags with numbers; this helps me keep track of their health and how many babies they produce. The day after the lambs are born and after ensuring that they are nursing well, I dock the tails of the girls. Sheep are born with long tails. I leave the tails on the boys since they are going to be sold as soon as they are weaned anyway. I found that the elastrator, a tool that places a small, strong rubber ring to cut off circulation , causing the tail to fall off in a couple of weeks, works best for me. I can easily do it myself and there is no bleeding after it's done, so less chance of infection. The reason they are docked is that long tails can accumulate large amounts of manure in the wool, attracting flies that lay their eggs on them and then become maggots, not pretty. I like to leave an inch and a half to two inches, enough to cover the anus. When I dock them I also give them a shot of tetanus. Both hurt for a while, you see them laying down squirming with the pain but after a couple of hours they seem to forget they have the ring on.

I had a set of six year old twins (boys, human) come and stay at the farm for a week, one of them was fascinated with the lamb tails he would find. He went around the field and the pens looking for them. He had quite the collection by the time he left.

I had another set of triplets born two days ago, two boys and a girl. I have noticed that the boys keep trying to nurse but the mother pushes them away and won't let them nurse. Her milk bag is small. Maybe she knows she will not have enough for all three and has decided that she is only keeping the girl. Without proper nutrition and in this cold, newborns die really quickly. They are not able to maintain their body heat without the nutrition provided by the colostrum, the mother's first milk. I have milked her and bottle fed some of it to the boys. I have also been giving them a commercial milk replacer but I am already bottle feeding a couple more. It is a full time job, a bottle every four hours. These babies that have been abandoned are very persistent though, they try to feed off any mom that will let them. Sometimes they get lucky and find a mom that is distracted eating and thinks it's her own babies, by the time she realizes, they have already had a good drink. She butts them off with her head as soon as she does, hopefully that will keep them going until their next feeding. I leave them in the pen with the mother in hopes that she changes her mind and decides to be a mother to them.

A more permanent solution presented itself the next day. A ewe had been in distress all day and had not been able to produce anything. When I went looking for her I found her laying in the field, I knew then, something was wrong. I was going to have to help her. Thankfully that day a young man that comes to do the landscaping and odd jobs at the farm, was here, and I asked him, if he would help me. I needed him to hold her down for me to examine her, and take them out if I needed to. I came prepared with my gloves and lubricant. We lay her on her side and I had him hold her hind legs so she won't kick me or try to get up. I go in, and just as I suspected, the baby is across. I have a hard time trying to get it in the right position to get it out. When I finally do, I can see why she could not birth it, not only was it across but it must have been dead for a while. I go in again to make sure I got it all and sure enough I feel another set of little legs, much smaller than the one I just pulled out, maybe a third the size of the first one. This one must have died months ago, its tiny and already decomposing. I clean her up as much as I can and we bring her up to the pens where I find a stall to put her in. I am going to need to get her some antibiotics and a shot of Pitocin to ensure the placentas are expelled. I saw one but not the other, if they are not expelled she is sure to get an infection. So here I have a mom with no babies and two babies with no mom. Why not try and bring them together! I had read in one of my vet books that sometimes a ewe will adopt a baby and I was going to do everything I could to try to have this mom take the job of raising the abandoned babies from me. Her milk bag is large and swollen with colostrum that I know my babies will love.

I drive off to the vet's office, I have already called ahead and explained what happened and he will have what I need along with instructions at the office for me. The vet's office is not far, I like the drive there through country roads. In the spring they are beautiful, flanked with fields on either side of the road, planted with neat rows of plants that become white puffs of cotton in the summer. I pick up the meds and rush back. As soon as I arrive, I go straight to the stall. I am to give her a shot of Pitocin and one of antibiotics today, and another one of antibiotics to be administered tomorrow. I restrain her and find a spot in her hindquarters, where there is large muscle mass and give it, in a quick motion, like throwing a dart. I pull back a little to make sure I did not hit a vein and then push the meds in. As soon as this is accomplished, I set about to test my plan.

I bring my babies in, they are hungry, and I grab hold of the mom and hold her by the neck as if giving her a hug and call the babies. They come, they are used to me since I have been feeding them, I push them towards her milk bag and they start suckling on her loudly as if they know they need to get as much as they can in a hurry. The mom struggles with me to try to get away but I won't let her until they are full. I leave them together in the stall so they can get to know each other and I will return in four hours for another feeding. We do this, tackle the mom every four hours for the next two days and on the third day I just put my hand on her neck and she does not move and lets the babies nurse. Yess!!! I did it, or we did it, with the babies, we found a new mom. When I check them on the fourth day, they are laying together as a family. She is a mother again and they are happy with their bellies full and the mother's warmth by their side. They look at me with a smile of satisfaction on their face, but they don't run to me anymore like they did when they were hungry, they have found their mother.

A mother, being a mother is the hardest jobs I have ever had to do. Children don't come with instructions and I did not have a lot to go on, when it came to mothering. My mother had left when I was little and my stepmom had not been a model of motherhood to me. So when it came my turn to be a mother,

I had to wing it. At least I had, had plenty of practice when it came to caring for a baby. Like I mentioned before my mom brought one home every year and my stepmother continued the tradition. I had learned to feed a baby and change a diaper, the cloth ones with the pins on the side, since age eight. I loved caring for the babies because I could stay in la amaca all day, swinging back and forth and I did not have to sweep or do dishes or laundry, it was great. I got so good at it that the babies would cry if my stepmom tried to take them away from me.

I had a break from babies when I moved to the States, until my sister Lore had her first, when I was fifteen. I was so excited; I had missed caring for babies and would ride my bike to her house after school to help her with her baby. It had been a boy, Christopher, loved him so much, I would rather stay home and take care of him, instead of going to a party. That's saying a lot because I use to love to dance, wait, I still do. She soon got pregnant with her second child(very fertile, family trait) I was hoping for a girl this time, I prayed hard for one, but no, another boy.

A year later, and it was my turn. I was eighteen years old (too young to be a mom). It was a hot and humid August and I could not find a comfortable position for me to rest. I sat in a recliner at night to try to get some sleep; I could no longer lay flat in a bed. I was afraid but I knew it had to come out. If I could relax, I knew my body knew what to do. I had heard so many horror stories of women suffering in agony for days before they delivered their babies. I was anxious for the day to come, and at the same time I was filled with trepidation. My lower back had been aching all afternoon, and it was now eleven at night, when a gush of warm water went down my leg. The time had come; there was no going back now. I was finally going to meet this little person that would change my life forever. Brought with it a new role for me, one I was afraid, I would not play well. I was overjoyed at the chance to try anyway; I would give it my best chance.

I woke him up after I had called my sister and asked her what to do. She was a nurse, and I trusted her judgment more than any doctor. She had said for me to go to the hospital right away. We lived in a one bedroom apartment we had gotten together when I was about five months pregnant. My baby's daddy was just a boy too, nineteen. We had started dating when I was about fifteen. He had been my first love, my only boyfriend. He had been with me through the death of my sister Daisy, and I had taken refuge in our love, I thought at the time it was the only good thing I had left. We now worked at a nursing home together as nursing assistants. I fell even more in love with him when I saw how gentle he was with his patients. He used to take care of this lady, Mrs. Potter, she screamed all day whatever word you put into her head in the morning, banana, was usually the word he would pick for her. We would hear it loudly in that hall all day long. I watched him braid the old ladies hair and play around with them as he cared for them. They all loved him as I did. He was shy and gentle and sweet.

When we arrived at the hospital, they made me sit in a wheelchair and wheel me to labor and delivery, I told them I could walk but they did not listen to me. When the doctor came in to examine me, he told me I was ten centimeters dilated and that I would be taken in right away, I was ready to deliver. A half an hour later the cries of my little girl pierced the halls of Melrose-Wakefield hospital's maternity ward at three in the morning. (A few years later I worked in that same hospital for a number of years, including the nursery).

I had thought that when I had her, I would automatically be flooded with motherly feelings, but I did not feel anything. I kept looking at my baby and could not believe that she was

really mine. All I wanted was for my sister to come; she would know what to do. Many people say that all moms think their baby is the most beautiful baby in the world, I didn't. She was tiny, with a full head of black hair sticking up. Everyone that saw her would comment on it, "Will you look at the hair on that baby". I thought that maybe there was something wrong with me, that this was not how it was supposed to be. In hindsight, however, there is no one way things are

supposed to be, or one way in particular a new mother feels. It's different for everybody every time. We must do the best we can with what we get. We took her home two days later. I spent that first month of her life trying to get used to this new role I had been blessed with. I had always wanted a baby girl but never thought I would get one because I wanted one so bad. When my sister had her boys I had prayed each time for them to be girls and was disappointed each time and so I had given up on the idea and had resolved myself to the boy I was sure I was going to have. I finally had a living doll, the little girl, I had always dreamed of having. Unfortunately, I did not get enough time to spend bonding and getting to know her like I wish I had. I had to return to work in a months' time. I would leave her at the sitters at six am and not be back till four or four thirty, and then it was rush to get home and dinner and it was bed time. I only got a couple of hours spent with my baby every day. Not enough and that is time I can never get back.

The struggle to mother my child was made even harder when her father and I split up; we were too young and unprepared for all we had taken on. We both wanted to go on different paths in life and ended up going separate ways. It was her and I for a long time. Many times I felt like there was no place for me. I did not fit in with people my age, they were in college or having a blast partying. I did not fit with other mothers both because they had their husbands and they did not want me hanging out with them.

So it was the two of us against the world. We had our rough times and I was lonely at times, for it was years before I dated again.

But we were happy. I enjoyed being a mother and dressing up my princess in the dresses I learned to make for her. Perhaps one day, I would be given the chance to play the role again and be a mother one more time and hopefully, I do better that time.

Special Delivery

My days were gray
My nights were cold
My heart was numb, I had no joy!
Two years went by
And then two months
When hope was gone
A package came
It was august six at three am

The sun came up to warm my heart!
And for me to see
What the night had brought!
There was a tag that read
"To mend a broken heart"
I could clearly see
It was addressed to me

I reached inside and there I saw...
Little eyes looking back at me!
My days were busy
Chasing little feet
It was not easy
My nights were sleepless
With fevered heads
And never ending diapers!

The years went by and by
Now you are grown and gone
To my heart joy you've brought
You mended a broken heart
Now is time for you to find
Joy and warmth
For your own little heart!

Sonia Lopez
June 2011

A Wife

I thought at first, I would just leave a couple of pages blank under this heading. I have been married more than once and failed each time. Nonetheless, from each failure, I have learnt what not to do. And also what I don't want.

Do not rush! This has always been a hard thing for me. I am not a very patient person. Once I have decided on a course, I like to get going as soon as possible, and get what I need along the way. This of course, does not always pen out. The ideal thing when setting on a new course, (I have tried this and works so much better) is to know where you are going, how you are going to get there, why you want to go, and what you will need for the trip.

Life is a journey, having a traveling companion can make the trip idyllic but it could also make it into a trek uphill. Hence, the importance of taking the time to find one that is well suited to you.

The first wise thing to do would be to know you. What you want out of life? Where you want to go? Do you travel light? Do you like to try out new things, visit new places? Or do you prefer to stay close to home? Do you like being around people all the time or do you prefer solitude and quiet? Does sharing come easy to you? Are you a morning person? Are you organized? Do you procrastinate? Do you get along with your family? Do you try to resolve conflict or avoid it? It took me a long time to figure out what I wanted. Maybe because I was never asked what I wanted and learnt to accept what was handed to me without question. From a very young age I was thought to put the needs of others ahead of mine. What my preference was did not matter, what I wanted was not important. I was not important. I am grateful to have learned to put the needs of others ahead of mine for it is easy to become selfish and think only of one's needs, but I have also learnt that in order to take good care of others, we have to first, take care of ourselves. And to do that we need to know what we need, what you want.

In retrospect, a major impediment that hindered my ability to pick a partner for my journey was my inability to know my own worth.

In Hispanic culture, like many around the world, a woman's worth is largely measured by her chastity. On the outside they might say different but the idea that a girl is to be pure until the day of her wedding is deeply rooted and was very prevalent amongst the people I grew up around. For men is different, their worth is measured by the amount of money they can make. There is a double standard when it comes to sexuality. Men are given ample leeway when it comes to having premarital sex, it won't affect the opinion others have of him.

I had my first child out of wedlock, I had been devalued, and this is what society, those around me, had thought me. People's opinion of us can greatly affect the opinion we make of our selves. I had internalized the concept others had of me, I believed I was not as worthy as other women. I remember one time this "friend of the family" was very interested, in this particular young man, becoming her son in law. She thought I was interested in him as well so she pulled me aside one day and said "mosquita muerta, tu crees que un muchacho como ese se va fijar en una mujer como tu, con hijos ya?" her words cut me deep, I was just a young girl, must have been twenty then, but what she said, was what a lot people thought, they just did not have enough reason to voice their opinion.

Believing myself not good enough, when the chance at marriage came along I felt fortunate to have been proposed to. It happened around the time my daughter was four years old. I met him through a friend at a picnic. She introduced us, he was a hard working young man from my country. She told me "you need to meet this guy, he seems nice and he is in a rush to get married" that should have been my first warning flag but I did not pay much attention to the comment. See, from the very beginning it was wrong, he wanted a wife (whatever that meant for him) not me. It just so happened that I was a young woman with hopes and dreams of having a home and a family of my own instead of just being single mom. But I was not what he wanted, he just settled for me, maybe because he did not want to wait for what he wanted. Two weeks before the wedding he told me though, and I admit that it was my fault for not having turned and walked away at the time. He got really quiet one day and said "I don't know why it always happens to me that the women I like already have kids". This really hurt, to have him say it, that I was not good enough .He thought he had been generous to have made the offer to me. He felt he was doing me a favor by marrying me. I told him we did not have to go through with it, that it was ok, that we should not get married if he did not think I was the one for him, that I totally understood. When I told him this though, he changed, started saying that he loved me and that it would all work out and he convinced me or rather I let myself get convinced that maybe it was the cold feet that some say people get. I wanted to believe that he loved me and that it would all work out in the end. I thought he would be happy when he saw what a good wife I could be.

He had let me know what his assessment of my worth was and by me accepting him as my husband, I too, had accepted his assessment of me, the worth he had assigned to me.

After the wedding I tried very hard to be what I thought was a "good wife". I kept the house clean, made sure to have dinner ready when he got home. Do his laundry and iron for him. I also had to work full time and since he managed the finances I gave him my paycheck. He would only let me have ten dollars a week for bus fare. We only had one car and it was a stick shift and I did not know how to drive standard, so I had to take the bus and the T to get to work and to drop my daughter off at preschool. We were saving for a house, he said, so I did not mind the sacrifices we had to make. Soon after we were married we decided to have a baby, he had told me he wanted one and I did not want to wait too long. My daughter was already in preschool and I did not want there to be a big age difference between the children so five or six months after we were married I got pregnant. By the time the baby was due to arrive we had purchased a two family home in Somerville, Massachusetts, in the Boston metro area. It was during a blizzard in the winter of ninety six that he made an entrance into the world. I had a false alarm a couple of weeks before and had to go back home. I was afraid the baby would come fast like my first one and I did not want to deliver in the car, on the way to the hospital, so I was very nervous about it. This time I was sure it was the real deal, the pains were stronger and I was only ten days from the due date I was given. My husband did not want to wait though; he dropped me off at the hospital with my sister Norma who had told me to call her because she wanted to be there when the baby came. He left me at the hospital at three am and the baby was born at seven, so he was not there when he arrived, my baby was handed to my sister and I told her to go with him and make sure that he did not get switched. We were both crying, not because of the pain but because he was so beautiful and we were so happy and grateful he was ok, we named him Micah, like a prophet in the Bible. Everything had gone well so I was discharged home the next day. When I got there, the first thing he told me was that he had no clean shirts for work the following day. I could not believe it! I, had just had a baby for this man without him by my side, and all he could think of was that I had not done the laundry.

Besides the lack of affection and support from my husband I really enjoyed this baby. I was really ready for him to come and had taken three months maternity leave to be home with him and I never went back full time after he was born. I went back part time, three nights a week.

My daughter was really excited about being a big sister and was a big help by bringing me whatever I needed for him. She had started kindergarten so she was gone most of the day while I was home with him. My days were very busy caring for both my children and the house in addition to my job. I was discouraged though, I had imagined that it was going to be different with this baby because I had a husband, but I felt more alone than ever. He did not want to do any of the things that most parents do together when they are expecting. I painted his room on my own, it was a mint green and I put a border on the top with bears on it. I convinced him to buy the crib even though he kept insisting that we should just let him sleep with us. He finally bought it but I had to put together by myself. My daughter was my only little helper, she had her own room but she moved into his room most nights. There was a futon in his room where she made her bed.

A few months after, I was scheduled for a doctor's visit and I had made a decision, I did not want to have any more babies somehow I knew I would be raising them on my own and I did not want to have so many that I could not care for them. I told the doctor that I wanted to have my tubes tied; I wanted to be sure I was not going to get pregnant again. He did not want to because I was just twenty- four years old, he kept insisting that what if I lost one to illness or an accident but I convinced him that having another baby would not bring back the one I lost. I finally convinced him, no more babies for me, and no more husbands either for what he had always wanted had finally arrived.

We used to go out to dinner on Sundays after church, sometimes he asked friends to join us. Some friends of ours had recently had a sister of theirs move from their country to Massachusetts and my husband asked her to join us for dinner, I did not think anything of it because we regularly had others join us, and I was too busy feeding and caring for my daughter to notice anything. He must have fallen in love with her and I had no idea. He started being ruder than usual, upset at things for no apparent reason. One day he outright told me he was sorry he had married because I was used goods, yes he used those words, he told me "why don't you leave so I can marry a clean woman, a virgin, like I have always wanted". At the time I really did not know he had one picked out. I told him I would leave, but that I would leave when I was good and ready, I think that was the first time I stood up for myself and to him. Every so often he would ask, "Are you leaving yet?" Somehow his words had ceased to hurt me anymore, I was numb, I had disconnected my

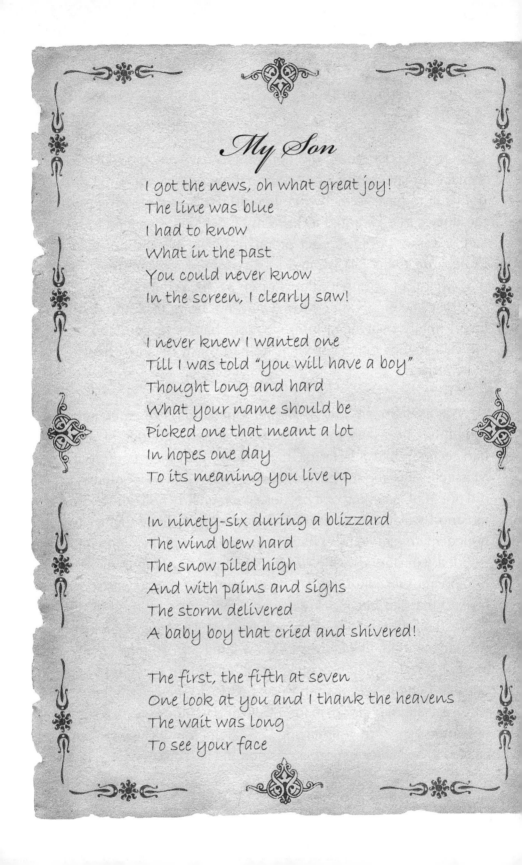

My Son

I got the news, oh what great joy!
The line was blue
I had to know
What in the past
You could never know
In the screen, I clearly saw!

I never knew I wanted one
Till I was told "you will have a boy"
Thought long and hard
What your name should be
Picked one that meant a lot
In hopes one day
To its meaning you live up

In ninety-six during a blizzard
The wind blew hard
The snow piled high
And with pains and sighs
The storm delivered
A baby boy that cried and shivered!

The first, the fifth at seven
One look at you and I thank the heavens
The wait was long
To see your face

To hear your cries
To count your toes
To kiss your cheeks!

My heart swelled
As I watched you grow
Caring, tender and sweet!
The time has flown
My little boy is soon a man
My son by chance
My friend by choice!

Your Mom always ....

heart, and I did not care anymore. I was thinking more of how I would manage when the time came for me to leave. I started saving and I also enrolled in a community college to try to get a degree in nursing but it was too much. The kids, the house, my job, I would just have to make do with what I had. The next time we argued and I don't even know what about and he asked again when I was going to leave, I took the kids and what I could put in the car and I left. Playing the part of a wife I guess is one that I just can't seem to get right.

I had not done my homework, I had not known who I was, I had not taken the time to get to really know him, and I had ignored the warning signals. I had not stood up for myself from the beginning so he had stood over me.

What I have learnt from being married is that it is the union of two lives. When you marry, you don't just join him but all who are already joined to him, his family and his friends. It is a good idea to get to know them too. What I have also learnt is what I don't want.

* I don't want someone to control everything I do.
* I don't want someone who thinks marriage is the end of fun.
* I don't want to be with someone who thinks he can still act like he is still single after marriage.
* I don't want to be the extension of someone else.
* I don't want to stop spending time with friends and family because I am married, of course It will not be the same or the same amount but some spouses want to have you to themselves and don't want you to spend any time with anyone else and that creates resentment.
* I want to share my life not live for someone else.

* If I cook, clean, do the laundry, I do it out of love. We share our life and our chores. I don't do it because I have to, or because it is expected of me but because I want to.
* I don't want to be taken for granted and unappreciated.

My slumber

Could not wait
Gave in to despair!
Thought I never find
Someone my world to share
Ignored my worth, till it was
    too late!

Gave my heart away
To those that never cared!
Could not be seen, was never heard
I was a thing put on display

My heart turned into stone
Slumber became my home
Why did you have to come?
To wake me up and then be gone!
You called my name, I thought I heard
From afar I can only stare

To pass the time I count my sheep!
Wish I could go back to sleep!
And not know what is amiss
Pick up my stone, accept my home
Say good night without a kiss...

Sonia Lopez
December 7, 2012

A Friend

$\mathcal{B}$eing a friend is like playing a supporting role, you let the other person be the main character and you take a back seat. Real friends are hard to find and it is hard to be one. It requires commitment. You have to give more than what you take. The ones that only take from you are not really your friends. If you only take from others, you are not a real friend. The Bible says "a true friend shows love at all times, and is a brother who is born for times of distress". When we count our friends we see, there are not many, we would call a "true friend" for there are degrees of friendship. We may have some we love to spend time with, they are fun, interesting. We might meet for dinner or lunch and catch up on the going on's in our lives. We might share a story or two. Only with a precious few, though, would we share our most inner thoughts with, our fears, our dreams. We know they would listen to us without judgment and offer alternatives we had not thought of. They are like coaches, watching the game, from the sidelines. They see our strengths and our weaknesses; they can see the game better than we can. True friends encourage us and urge us on. A true friend is not afraid to tell you what you are doing wrong, even if you don't like it. A true friend helps you see yourself in a better light. Time and distance cannot hold true friends apart, they travel in the heart.

I know how important having a friend can be, but for a time, after my husband left me at the farm on my own with Mickey I went without any real friends. The ones I had were far away and I had not taken the time to make new ones. I wanted to wallow in my loneliness. I wanted to keep the emptiness I felt to myself. I did not want anyone to feel sorry for me, so I indulged in my isolation. The animals were my therapy, I often spoke to them. I liked the fact that they did not judge. There were days I did not even look at a mirror, I had let myself go. The animals did not seem to mind my disarray. They were happy when they saw me coming and they welcomed me. I kept busy and did not care.

I knew it was time to come out, to make new friends and to live again. This was a hard thing for me to do, for most days I did not like the human race. I knew, however, that I could not stay away from them forever, it was not healthy, or so I heard and I had my son. I did not want him to think I was crazy, I would make an effort to find new friends and talk to people. The first thing I did was pray for a friend before I set in search of one.

It did not take long for my prayer to be answered. An older couple had moved to the area from Florida, Samuel and Delia, and they were attending my church meetings. I sensed that she was in need of friends like I was. Many of her friends had been left behind and she was in need of new friends too. We started spending more and more time together. She would come on

Therapy

Have you ever felt so much pain in your chest?
And you look down to see
A gaping hole, where your heart used to be
Do you ever feel that no matter how deep you
   breathe?
You cannot get enough air?
And no matter how tired you are,
You cannot sleep?
If Diazepam, Lorazepan or Peter Pan from
   neverland
Ever been your closest friend, raise your hand!

Do you ever feel like you just got a "D?"
Disappointed
Defeated
Deflated
Demoted
Disoriented

Do you ever get up in the morning?
And think, just one more day...
Do you ever put a smile?
Over your pain and sorrow
And think, maybe tomorrow...
Do you ever feel like therapy is no longer working?

Hope you never do
But if you ever do
Just repeat the wise words
Of a fish named Dory

"Keep on swimming, what do we do?
We keep on swimming"

Mondays and help me wash and pack eggs for me to deliver. She enjoyed the peace of the country and we would take walks through the trails at the back of the property when all the eggs from the weekend had been washed and packed. There were a few acres of wooded areas behind the main house. The trails had been woven to go around and through the woods with streams that snaked the property and went over small bridges that had been built to go over the streams. She talked to me as if I was a daughter to her. She listened to me and gave me council when she thought I needed it. She was the one that pointed out to me that perhaps I needed to take better care of myself. She suggested that a haircut might be in order. And you know that when a woman cuts her hair she is about to change her life, and that is what happened. It snowballed from there. After getting the much needed haircut, I realized that I had put on some unwanted pounds; I had eaten my way through my sorrows. It was around that time that I read an article in the Awake magazine that talked about five things you could do to improve your health and your life. It talked about proper nutrition, exercise, rest, and spirituality, can't remember the fifth one but I know it started me thinking and setting goals for me, to live healthier. Someone had snapped a picture of me and I was so disappointed when I saw it, I vowed I would change. I could not change the fact I was getting older but I did not have to be fat. My friend Delia and her daughter would go to weight watcher's meetings and would talk about ways of eating better and counting calories. I did not go to their meetings but I would put into practice what they learned. I wanted to join a gym to try to get more exercise in but I was limited with time and money. Joining a gym can be expensive and I had done it in the past, gone a few times and then stopped but ended up paying for the year. I could not do that again. I was so far from any gyms here in the country anyway; I would have to find another way. One day while going through old video cassettes I came across one my sister in law had given to me many years back. It was a twenty minute kickboxing workout. I started doing it three times a week and watching what I ate. I have a sweet tooth I had been indulging a little too much, so I had to cut back on that. It was really hard at first; I had to make myself stick to my plan. When I started seeing results it gave me the push I needed to go on. And it was all thanks to my new friend who had taken a real interest in me and pointed out to me what I neglected to see.

I had prayed for a friend but I guess I must have needed more help than I thought for ended up getting two. First Delia, she was not just a friend but had become like a mother to me. Then another friend came to my life. She was a young woman going through a divorce, my expertise by now. She had some family in North Carolina and was staying with them. Here was my opportunity to give back, to be a friend to somebody else. And she was someone I could go out with for entertainment. All the other friends I had made were married, and I did not want to intrude on them, I spent time with them in the day when their husbands were at work but in the evening or weekends I had no one to hang out with. This new friend needed me too; it felt great to be of help to someone else. She spent a lot of time at the farm with me and got along great with Mickey. He loved having people around; I guess I had not been much fun for quite some time.

Maybe the farm had become therapy to her as it had been for me. She was a beautiful young woman, a lot younger than me; she was in her late twenties. She was full of energy, a little too much. Sometimes when she came over for a weekend she would want to stay up for a long time and talk endlessly. I am not used to staying up anymore, I love to sleep and I have to get up early to take care of the animals. I found the solution though, a little wine and a boring movie and she is out like a light. To have my friend Jessie around feels like having a little sister again. I love the fact that, even though she is a city girl, she is not reluctant to put on a pair of rubber boots and join me in the mud to help me do my chores. She is an animal lover. Maybe that is why we get along so well. She has a little dog, he is black and small, looks like a little black bear. She takes him everywhere she goes. His name is London. He likes the farm because he can be off his leash and he can run free with my dog Lily.

Her coming to spend the weekends gives me something to look forward to. I now have someone to go places with. She has many friends so I am meeting new people all the time and going places I would have never gone to. We like to meet for coffee at Starbucks at Baxter Village in Fort Mill. We would sometimes go for walks in the trails they have there. Having to go out to different places with her, helps me in my resolution of changing my life a bit. I'm forced to make myself look presentable, because I would not want to embarresss my new friend

My Best Friend

$\mathcal{T}$hey say a man's best friend is his dog, I think it must be a woman's too. When I was a little girl we always had dogs. The first one I remember was a white long hair dog named Capullo, he was a big dog and he was married to a little Black hair dog named Zuki. Together they made a whole bunch of puppies. We were allowed to keep two of them, Duke and Boliche. Boliche became mine, we went everywhere together. I remember one time I made the mistake of getting into a field and did not notice a cow that had just had a calf, they are very protective of their babies, she came charging after me running with her horns pointed straight at my back and I remember Boliche running in front of it dancing side to side to give me time to jump the fence and escape the sure death I would have had, had she gotten me first. He was my constant companion and protector. I never knew life without a dog.

When I moved to the states I lost the friendship you can only have with the four legged kind and for many years I thought I would never be able to have one again. Even though I always wanted to have one, I never thought I would be able to, until we moved to the farm. There was plenty of space here and she could guard the farm. I never set about getting one though because I knew what a big responsibility it is to have one. It is like having another child so I never asked my husband if we could have one.

I was watching a movie one time and I saw a dog in it and thought that if I ever had one, I wanted one just like her. It was a movie with Will Smith; he had a German Shepherd dog, a girl. The movie was "I Am Legend" I did not like the movie too much but that dog stayed with me. I don't even think I told anyone about it, but someone must have heard me because a few months after, my husband came home with a puppy, A German shepherd little girl with floppy ears and the same coloring as the one in the movie. It was his dog however, and he would take her everywhere he went, but in my heart she was mine on the day she arrived.

On the day he made his announcement that he was leaving, one of the things that went through my mind was that he would take my Lily with him. Alexis had picked the name for her. I did not want to see her go. I did not say anything though in hopes that he would just leave her. She was a year old now and for the past month she had stayed away from him. He had been angry the weeks leading to his departure and on one of those days he had taken a broom and beaten her with it. I don't remember what she had done but it was not worth getting a beating for it. I had been shocked that he would do that, I had not gotten close because he seemed like he would hit anyone that got in his way, he was so angry and I did not want to be next. I made sure she had no injuries from it but I think since then, she stopped being his dog and became mine, not just in my heart but in hers too. She has been a wonderful friend. She has kept me company all these years that I have spent alone in the farm. Where ever I go, she goes. She warns me when anyone approaches the farm and lays close when I am out doing my chores. When I go out in the evening to gather the sheep she goes with me and she knows to get them in the pens before it gets dark.

She never judges me, loves me and knows exactly when I need some kisses and company. She looks at me with those brown eyes and I know she can see all the way inside my soul like no human can. With those same eyes she comforts me with the wisdom of words unsaid that ring loud and clear inside my mind and heart.

She understands loss and betrayal and having your heart broken.

She is a girl, after all, and all girls will have their heart broken a few times before every story is done with.

She fell in love with a chocolate lab she met at the end of road. It was early spring, the fields were in bloom with wild flowers and songs filled the air with stories of never ending love. The trees were crowned with pink promises of future happiness. He had smelled her scent and come from afar, he told her he could not believe how beautiful she was, that he could not sleep, that the images of her running through the fields tormented him at night, she was the last thought at dawn when finally the fatigue of running after her in his dreams overpowered him. When he awoke all he could think of was of being with her, he could not even eat, he had to see her, he would run to her as soon as he was let off his leash, he would find her and they would be together forever. The warm afternoon breeze would carry his letters of love to her and she too fell in love with a passion she never thought possible, she had never met a more handsome dog, his eyes were the color of honey and he was made of chocolate. She had tried to resist for she had heard that chocolate is poisonous to dogs but she could no longer refrain herself, even if she died, she had to taste the sweetness he offered. I saw her going to him one afternoon when I was pulling into our drive, I called after her, told her he would just break her heart, that he would take what he wanted and leave but she could no longer hear me, all she heard was the song he sang to her of his love so great. It was already dark when she came back, she seemed quiet and reserved, she could not believe that this was all love was, so fleeting. He had given her something, she was not sure what it was, he told her it would grow with time, that he could not see her anymore. The crazed excitement had not allowed her to be still, she had felt like she could fly and explode with happiness, nothing had mattered but being with him, and now all she felt was a paralyzing calm, was it all an illusion, she wondered if she had been under a spell, at least now she could sleep, that's all she really wanted to do. Waiting for him had kept her up so many days and nights, she was tired and spent. She would sleep and think of him no more. When she awoke the next day, she could not believe how hungry she was, as if she had not eaten in days. Perhaps it was the emptiness he had left behind. No matter she would eat and fill the void until she was fat, and fat she seemed to be getting, more and more each day. All she did for days and weeks was eat and sleep to heal her broken heart.

A pang woke her up one night, a pain so great she thought she would die. Maybe it was something she ate, she tried to get out of the porch so she could relieve herself, maybe that would help, but she had been locked in at night, she scratched the door, tried to wake me up, but I only heard it in a faraway dream. It was the cries that woke me up, the tiny cries of one cold and scared. I came out to the porch and found it, it was a black little sausage, blind and cold and crying. Lily looked at it trying to figure out what it was, it had come out of her, she had not meant to dirty the porch, it seemed to be calling to her but she did not know what to do. I dried her and carried it to the garage where I had prepared a box for I knew what was coming even if she did not. I put the little one in and told her to get in the box with her. The little one soon found in her mother's belly the warmth she had left inside and something to fill her mouth. She was later joined by four others that fought for their mother's love and nipples. She could not believe what had happened. They were beautiful like he had been. Was this what he had given her and said in time would grow? She only wished he would be here with her to see what their love had made.

Small World

We were so excited when the chicks became hens and started laying. The first eggs to be laid were small; we used to call them practice eggs. Each day I would find more and more. When I found our first blue egg we were even more excited. I saved it for my employer, it almost looked like a robin's egg, and it was so small. Soon enough though, we had more eggs than we could consume or give away. My employer decided to order egg boxes and told me to sell whatever we had left over at a farmers market in charlotte. I would bring them Saturday morning and they would sell really quickly.

We package them to show off all the colors we produced, white, brown and blue. People loved the look and they said they could not eat store bought eggs after trying ours. The difference was really great not only in taste but in color. The yolks were almost orange, and the taste absolutely delicious! We could not keep the farmers market supplied, they would always run out.

My employers had also introduced her eggs to specialty stores and chefs she knew. They used her eggs in cooking demos. We were soon in high demand so we had to get more hens, so we ordered two hundred more chicks. Hens usually start laying at around five to six months of age, so by the following year

our production had really taken off. Spring is the natural time for hens to reproduce and is then that they lay the most eggs. That spring we had more eggs than we could sell, we needed a new store that would sell our eggs.

My employer told me about a small Italian store in her neighborhood that specialized in selling fresh products, like pasta that was made in the store, and fresh breads. She thought our eggs would sell well there. She had brought the owner our eggs to try and he had agreed to sell our eggs in his store. I was to bring our first delivery to them. We had gotten crates that made transportation easy and had a sticker that displayed our signature look of the three color eggs on the logo.

I had the address, it was on Providence road in downtown Charlotte, and even though it was in the middle of a big city when you arrived you felt like if you were in another part of the world. It was a brick building, a quaint little store with old world charm. When I opened the screened door and a small bell that was attached to it would sound as you pushed the door in. The floor was wood and worn down by the many years of use. There were wooden barrels next to the door used as tables that held freshly made chunks of bread on a platter with olive oil and valsamic vinegar for dipping for their patrons to sample, I sampled every time I came. The aroma was incredible, rosemary, oregano, parsley, basil, garlic it was all in the air as soon as you walked in. They had two large glass display counters. The first one on the right as you came in; it was filled with all kinds of processed meats that they would slice to order along with many deli cheeses. On the left was another counter with freshly made breads, pastas, olives, stuffed peppers, pickled artichokes and all kinds of homemade delicacies that left my mouth watering.

I take my crate to the back of the store where a young man takes it from me and tell me to wait for the check, he goes up a short flight of steps and tells someone in there to write the check and the amount it is for, he comes down and starts putting our eggs in the refrigerator where they are going to be displayed with one of the cases open so people can see the colors of the eggs. I look up again at what must be an office. There is a little window on it and a license plate on display along with photographs of what must be the family and employees of the store. It's a Massachusetts license plate, that's a coincidence! I still think of Massachusetts as my home, I guess because that's where I have lived the longest. A man comes out of the office with my check in his hand, he seems very familiar but I can't remember where I know him from. He introduces himself as Tom, I give him my name and take my check to leave but as I turn I notice at the back of the store another face I know, he is cutting sheets of pasta into fettuccine or linguine. It's my ex brother in law. I cannot believe it, this store is the reason I moved to the Carolinas. My ex-husband and this Tom had worked together in Massachusetts in a store similar to this and had moved to the Carolinas to open a new store after we got divorced. I had known about the store but I never cared to learn the name or where it was and now here I was delivering my first egg delivery to it! Thank God at least I knew my ex-husband no longer worked with him but his brother obviously still did. What were the odds that I would be delivering eggs and the first store I deliver to would be this one! Small world!!

Divorce 101

*D*ivorce is hard even if you don't want to be with the person that at one time, you thought you could not live without. Divorce is hard even if divorce is what you want. Divorce with children is not just hard, it is painful for everyone.

The day I had put my children in the car and driven off, I had nowhere to go and no money. I was homeless with two kids. One of my brothers offered me a place to stay until I could figure out what I was going to do. I had meant only to stay with him and his wife for a couple of weeks but the weeks turned into a few months. I knew I had outlived my welcome, I could not blame them. I had been trying very hard to find an apartment where we could move into and that I could afford but had been unsuccessful. I asked my mother if we could stay with her until I found something and she took us in, she had no room for us though and I had to sleep on the floor but it was better than a shelter. We could not stay with her long though, my youngest brother who at the time was in psychiatric hospital was soon to be discharged home and my ex-husband threatenned to take my children away if I lived with my mother for fear my brother might harm them. I was at the end of my rope. The day he was let out of the hospital I found an attic apartment in Everett, it was small but full of charm and best of all, something I could afford. It was a one bedroom apartment with a small kitchen in the back. There was a back door from the kitchen that led to a porch. There were trees in the back yard and some of the branches hovered over the porch making it feel like you were in a tree house, I knew the kids would love that.

I did not have much, but it felt so good to finally have a place of our own. I bought a bed and a little red striped sleeper sofa for the living room, and a little TV for the kids. Soon our little tree house felt like a home. I enrolled the kids in school. It was going to be the first year of full time school for Mickey, pre-K and Alexis was going to be in fourth or fifth, I can't remember. It was walking distance from our apartment so that was nice. Mickey was not happy to go to school. Every morning he would complain of a stomach ache or make himself throw up so I would not send him or he would go to the nurse and I would get a call to come pick him up. It must have been very hard for him. He missed his father and our house in Somerville. His homesickness was aggravated even further when his father came to pick him up and kept him for the weekend. When he came back he would cry for a long time and would tell me he did not love me, that he loved his daddy more and that he wanted to live with him. It was a struggle every week, and it broke my heart to see him suffer. I would try to distract him with games we would play or we would watch Sponge Bob square pants together or the Thornberry's until he forgot or until the next time he went over to his father's, then I would have to start all over again.

It had been several months since I had left my house in Somerville. I had tried to get Mickey's dad to agree on our own to divide our assets. I wanted some money from my part of the house. I had worked just as hard as he had to get it and I felt I deserved to have something. It had been five years where I had had no control of my earnings, even if I spent on a slice of pizza I had to give an account for it, and I would have to listen to a sermon about eating the bread of laziness. It was not fair that he kept it all but he would not see it, and that frustrated me even more than not getting anything. I could not understand how somebody could be so unfair and think they were right. He once told me that the only contribution I had ever made for that house was that I swept it once in a while and that I would never get a nickel from him. It had been almost a year until I finally hired a lawyer to help me get a divorce and let the courts settle the division of our assets and establish child support. I remember I told him one time, "trate de arreglar las cosas contigo a la Buena, pero a la Buena no quieres pues hay te va a la mala". I had asked him for ten thousand dollars so I could have a start, but he had not even considered it. The court did not take long to order him to start paying child support and said he had to buy me out of my part of the house. We had purchased the house when the market was good and cheap, in five years the house had tripled in value. The court ordered him to pay me ninety thousand dollars, half of what the profit of the sale would bring. He gave me sixty with the promise that he would pay me the remaining thirty at the time of the sale. I never saw those thirty, but it was more than I ever hoped to get. I felt vindicated, and I was so glad I had not allowed him to do whatever he wanted with me, that I was able to defend myself and get what was mine. I think he thought I would not go through with it, that I was bluffing and I would not go to court. I was tired of being the victim, I was tired of him walking all over me, and I had let him. I used to be afraid of him and he knew it, but I was free now and I had enough to start fresh.

He was given every other weekend visitation. When he came to pick him up he would throw the child support money on the floor so I had to pick it up in front of him, I would smile at him and pick it up and thank him, I would not get angry, I would not give him that. He hated that of course. He soon re-married and wanted custody of my son. He had plans to move to the Carolinas and wanted to take my son with him. I imag-ined his lawyer told him that the only way he was going to get custody was if Mickey was neglected or abused so he called DSS and accused me of neglect and accused my eleven year old daughter of sexual abuse towards my son. I was investi-gated, the children had to be examined by their pediatrician and interviewed by a child psychologist. After a few weeks of visitations and interviews it was determined that there was no base for the allegations and the case was dismissed. I must ad-mit though, that after that whole year of being under constant stress, not knowing what I was going to do, being homeless and the court battles had taken its toll on me. I was not ok, mentally or emotionally, I felt drained, and after that entire struggle all I wanted to do many times was giving up and let him have him. Many times I question myself. What if he was right? What if he could provide a more stable environment for him? Especially now that he was married again, What if I was being selfish?

He moved to the Carolinas to open up the pasta business where I delivered the eggs to. He continued in his pursuit to get custody even if he changed tactics somewhat. He must have read me, the doubts I felt. When he called he would tell me how all he wanted was, what was best for my son. He sounded so sincere and my son seemed to miss his father so much, I felt like a terrible mother. I felt like I was making my child suffer but at the same time I could not imagine sending him off to another state and not seeing him on a regular basis. I felt torn. What was I to do? What was the right thing to do?

It was late afternoon when I crossed the George Washington Bridge in New York. I had decided the night before that perhaps a move was the right thing for me. I knew my ex was not going to let up in his pursuit to get custody. He claimed that he did not want his child to grow up without a dad, like he had to. I felt that it was more that he hated to have to pay child support but I gave him the benefit of the doubt. I hoped that he was being sincere and really wanted custody of my son because he loved him and wanted to be near him. I was giving him what he wanted, custody of my son, but I could not live without seeing him and being near to make sure he was ok. So my plan was to move to North Carolina, put my son at his door with his bags and find a place to live on the opposite side of town, find work, and see him on the weekends. Down deep in my heart I felt that he was not going to be able to do it, he had never taken care of him, it had always been me. I fed him, bathed him, bought his clothes, dressed him, took him to the doctor, I did not think he could do it and I wanted to prove it to him. The only way to do it was to let him try, or he would never let me have peace. I had never gambled but I was gambling now, and what I was putting on the table was one of the most valuable gifts I had received, my son.

I had stayed up late studying the map of Charlotte, it seemed like a big city, bigger than I had imagined. I found his address on the map and I put a circle around it. He lived on the west side of town so I decided I would live all the way in the east side of town. There was a hospital sign on the map near where I had been looking. Maybe I could get a job there. I had not got much sleep. I was excited and scared. I had never driven that far. The most I had done on my own had been to New York. I had always wanted to go on a road trip to place far away. It was everything back in the car again. I put in as much as I could fit into the car. Our clothes, some of the kids toys and the small TV I had gotten for the kids that had a DVD player. I had not told the kids yet and I was not sure what they were going to say. Mickey would probably be happy he was going to see his dad, my daughter Alexis was another story, she had friends at school and she was close to my family. We were going to a place where we knew no one, she probably would think I was crazy, and she would not be happy about it, that is why I did not tell her my plan. The kids were on Christmas break and my sister had invited my daughter shopping that morning, so I had dropped her off at her house. I went home and packed everything into the car while she was away. I told her I would pick her up at my sister's house later. I had printed a MapQuest printout of the directions to Charlotte and to his house that I had gotten from an envelope he had used to send the child support. I made sure I had all our documents and I had gone to the bank the day before to close my account. I took two thousand dollars in cash and the rest on a bank check. I would open an account in Charlotte when I arrived. It was December 30th when we left Massachusetts. Mickey was going to be seven the following week. I told him we were going on a trip and we were going to pick up Alexis from Tia's house and then go, but I did not tell him where the trip was to. I would tell them together. When I got there, I honked the horn and she came out and said bye to her aunt, my sister. I did not get out of the car, I did not want my sister or anyone to know yet or they might try to convince me otherwise and I had already made up my mind of what I was going to do and did not want to waste any more time. When she got in the car and saw that there was only enough room for her she looked at me and said "what is all this?" When she had put on her seat belt and we were on our way I told her "we are going on a road trip to North Carolina for Mickey to see his dad" and to this Mickey in the back in his booster seat said "Yeay". Alexis bombarded me with questions, for how long? What about school? I have things in my locker, what about grandma and Tia, when we going to see them? I tried to answer as vaguely as possible and I tried to make the trip sound like a fun adventure. I had brought with us a leapfrog book that had all kinds of interesting facts like the capitals of all the states and I soon got them into learning them as we drove on. I handed Alexis the printout of the directions and told her she was the copilot and she had to tell me where I was to switch roads and she did a great job of it, since I could not read and drive at the same time. Soon we were out of the Boston metro area headed south and the towns seemed to fly by, each mile took us farther and farther from this place where I had grown and had always said, especially at winter time, that one day I would leave and fly south, somewhere warmer. I was not flying, but the Carolinas were definitely warmer than this. It was the end of December and the worst of the winter was still to come. I did not know what was going to happen when we got there, when the kids fell asleep, and I did not have to pretend to be happy for them. I worried and wondered if I was making a big mistake and if maybe I should turn back. I knew for sure I had to turn back when I saw the welcome sign for Delaware, we were not supposed to go through Delaware. I must have taken a wrong turn. It was getting late anyway, I would find a hotel to spend the night and resume our adventure tomorrow.

We got up in the morning and went to get breakfast before we got on our way. We were soon back on course, and by midday we had reached Virginia. It was beautiful country, with sloping hills and valleys dotted with cattle and farms for miles and miles. It was beautiful but after a few hours behind the wheel and after a poor night's sleep, I was tired and I did not want to see anymore cows. All I wanted to see was the "Welcome to North Carolina" sign, but I just went on and on. It was getting late, the sun had already started its daily descent and no Carolina on the horizon, so we stopped for dinner at a country buffet. After we had our fill of barbeque ribs, mac and cheese, green beans and biscuits, we felt more Southern and we were ready to take the road again. One stop to the bathroom and it was back on the road again. I was anxious to make it to Charlotte before it got too late. The kids were tired too. They already knew all the capitals and did not want to play anymore. Finally the sign I had waited for welcomed us to North Carolina and I breathed a sigh of relief. It was hours however before we reached charlotte, almost midnight. I did not know much about charlotte, just what I had read a couple of nights before we left and what I could gather from the map. I saw a Hampton Inn in downtown and that is where we headed. It was now New Year's Eve and I hoped I could get a room at this time of the night. Thankfully we did and we were happy to get in bed. The hotel was noisy with people celebrating the New Year and I don't know what happened but we were awaken by the fire alarms a couple of hours after we went to sleep. We had to stand outside the hotel until they cleared the alarm. That was our welcome to Charlotte.

In the morning I called Mickey's dad and told him we were in Charlotte and I would be coming by in an hour to deliver his kid. I don't think he believed me, but in an hour I had found his house. I had sat Mickey down that morning to explain to him that he would be staying with his father like he had wanted to. I asked him if he was sure he wanted to live with him instead of me and he said he was sure. I told him "ok then, we are going to his house now, you are going to live with him and Alexis and I are going to find a place to live around here and we can see you on the weekend ok?" He was so happy and excited to go see his dad, he had not seen him in a few months. I hoped he stayed happy, and I hoped I was doing the right thing. I did not want Mickey to hate me and blame me for keeping him away from his dad.

It went quickly; we stood at the door and rang the bell. When he opened the door, Mickey jumped into his arms, I handed him his suitcase, his birth certificate, social security card and immunization record. I told him to call me if he needed anything and told him I was staying in Charlotte for a while and that I would be picking him up on Saturday for the weekend. I tried to be businesslike and matter of fact. He looked at me as if he could not believe what was happening. When I got back in the car I was shaking and my heart was going a hundred miles per hour, I had done it, the hardest part was over. Now I would take it one day at a time. I would enjoy every minute I had with him when I had him and I would not have this fight anymore. I would concentrate on finding a place for my daughter and try to enjoy this new life I had come to in the South. I wanted peace.

We drove down to the place I had chosen on the map. I would have to find a hotel room near where I had decided I was going to live and I found another Hampton Inn in the town of

Matthews, near the hospital I had circled. We checked in and started getting to know the area. Tomorrow I would start looking for an apartment.

I still cannot believe what I did. It was the hardest thing I have ever done, to give up my child thinking that it might be the best for him even while my heart was breaking. It was the gutsiest gamble that paid off big in the end.

Building the Nest Again

*E*very week I made it a point to build up the nests. Hens love to scratch and toss things around and they always manage to throw all the nesting hay on the floor and I have to put new hay in for them. Something else they do is poop on their own nests. Sometimes they roost on the edge of the nest and while asleep they drop their messes where the next day they will lay their eggs. So it's a constant chore to make sure the nests are clean and have fresh hay, otherwise the eggs get dirty and it is hard getting the poop off of them.

I have had to rebuild my own nest many times too, yes I like scratching around too and I am an expert at making a mess of things.

When I arrived in Charlotte it was back to square one, I had to start all over again. The one good thing was that at least I did not have to worry about money this time. I still had the money from the sale of the house in Boston. After a couple of days in the hotel in Matthews I went looking for an apartment for us to live in. I should have taken my time but everything looked so nice and green and the apartments were so much better and easier to find than up North that I took the first one I looked at I think. It was a two bedroom with two bathrooms, something unheard of in Boston where almost all the houses are more than a hundred years old, and no matter how big the house or how many rooms it has, it only has one bathroom. And the closets, tiny! This apartment had a walk in closet in the master bedroom and real fireplace. I could not believe the rent either, five hundred and fifty! An apartment like this could have easy cost more than a thousand, so I paid six months up front and we moved in. my daughter would be going to middle school and the school was very close to the apartment complex, I think this was another reason I chose to move into this particular complex. I enrolled her in school the next week and soon we started settling in and getting to know the town. I had a lot of time by myself since my daughter was in school and would get lonely at times since we did not know anybody here but soon I found a job and got busy working and going places with my daughter. On the weekends we would go pick up Mickey and go places with them. That first year we bought season passes to Caro winds and spent fun times riding the coasters and playing in the water park. When I picked him up he would cling to me and did not seem too happy when I would return him home on Sunday. His father would call me many times to pick him from school because he was sick; when I got him he said he felt better. I would lie in bed with him and rub his back, he thought I had healing powers, he would say but I think it was that he missed me. He had never been separated from me for more than a couple of days and going with his dad for a couple of days was not the same as living with him. The stepmom that had seemed sweet when he came to visit was not the same anymore, he told me that she would leave him outside and he had to walk to his uncle's house until his dad got back from work but for me, not to tell his dad he told me, because he would get mad. I would be so upset at having to return him but I needed things to take their course and I wanted Mickey to see for himself where he wanted to live. I had custody by the court but I did not want to force him, I wanted him to want to live with me.

One day after work I went to a real state agency to see what was available in the area for houses. I wanted to see if I could get a more permanent place for us. I did not think I could get a house on my own but the real estate lady told me I was prequalified for an amount greater than what I thought I could afford. After looking at many houses, I found one with three bedrooms and two baths, with a good size yard. It was close to work and my daughter's school. I liked the layout of the house and the fact that it was under one hundred thousand dollars, with a good down payment, the mortgage payments would be almost as much as what I was paying for rent on the two bedroom apartment. I made an offer not thinking it was going to get accepted. I could not believe that I could have a house of my own. I had bought that house with my ex-husband in Boston but it never felt like my own. Two days later I had an answer, my offer had been accepted. We closed before the month was over. We would be moving in at the middle of May and school was out the first week of June. I wanted to make the house a home for me and the kids. I had left enough money to buy some furniture. My daughter and I had gotten beds for us but Mickey would just sleep with me when he came for the weekend. I wanted him to have his own room. I bought him a bedroom set and painted his room blue, his favorite color. When he came the next time he would have his own room.

School was out for the summer and I went to pick up Mickey from his father's house. I asked him if he wanted me to keep him for the summer and he said "yes, two months" I could not believe it!. We had fun that summer and somehow I felt that he would not be going back but it did not want to say anything prematurely. Mickey did not seem to want to go back either, so when the summer was coming close to an end and it was time to go back to school, when his father came to pick him up for a weekend. He returned him on Sunday and I asked him "So do you want me to enroll him in school here or are you going to take him?" he said "you enroll him" I said "ok but I will need all the papers I gave you" He looked kind of embarrassed for the first time since I had known him and said "my wife tore up the social security card, do you think you can order another one?" and that was that. I had put on my poker face, made a gamble and won. I had flown south for the winter, I had made a nest and had my chicks warm under our own roof and we were not lonely for long for in short my mother, my sister Lore, and one of my brothers came to visit and they too stayed.

My ex-husband never threatened to take my son again from me and my son never said he wanted to live with his dad again. In fact a year or so after we moved into our house his father stopped taking him for the weekend. He would just pick him up for the day and bring him back at in the evening.

Time to say good bye

*I*t is Spring again, a time of renewed hopes, a time when dreams are in bloom like the flowering trees. It is a time for change, for new life. It is a busy time at the farm. This is my favorite time of the year. I never tire of seeing my sheep bring new lambs into the world. This year is a special one for me for its going to be my last.

I have been at the farm now, five years, and it's time for me to leave, so I am trying to enjoy every minute I have left. Lambing season is almost over and I have counted seventy new lambs, all beautiful and all miracles. Mickey is finishing the eleventh grade and out here in the country there are very sparse opportunities for employment. It is my job to teach him to be a responsible member of society. Part of that is learning to provide for oneself. He needs a job and he will need to go to college in a year. It would be easier to do both in the city. I still have my house in Charlotte, that little nest I made for my children when I arrived in charlotte eleven years ago, it's been rented all this time and I have wanted to go back to it. It has been the only house I have ever wanted to go back to. I need to show it some love, fix it up a bit, it deserves it. It welcomed us at a time when I felt the most vulnerable. In it, I was able to gather my chicks together and keep them together and warm.

I miss spending time with my family too. This is wonderful job, but it is time consuming. The animals don't care that is the weekend, or a holiday, they need to be fed and care for all the time. If they are sick, you have to take care of them no matter the hour. The herd has gotten too big for me to handle and at times I have felt overwhelmed, especially when I have lost some to illness, something that is inevitable. Sheep don't do as well in warm climates like we have in South Carolina. They are susceptible to worms and it is very hard to maintain a healthy herd.

I am so grateful for this chance I've had to show my son how good life can be out here. How connected we can be to the land and the animals, I hope this experience stays with him and helps him when he has children of his own and he shares it with them. I am grateful that I was able to reconnect with this part of me that had been lost. When I leave I will be more whole than when I arrived. I have had time to heal and to make peace with the past.

Now, I have to show him how to survive in this world. Sometimes we forget that we won't always be here. I often wonder what he would do if something happened to me, if he would be ok, if I have given him the tools to make it. He has gotten too comfortable here. He does not want to leave. I am afraid that if I don't take him now he might have a harder time later.

He is afraid of change, yet change, is the one thing we can always count on. Nothing stays the same, everything is always moving. We are always changing. I want him to learn that with change comes opportunity. If we concentrate on what is gained instead of what is lost we will come out better at the end.

I want him to learn that what remains and what we never run out of, are the things that really matter, what we hold dear.

When we leave the farm, the farm will not leave us.

It will travel with us in our hearts!

"Spring has come"

It came at last!
The warmth to thaw my heart
An unwanted guest had come
Would not depart!
So dark, so cold a trap
Counted the days...froze in wait
You came at last
You held the door, you showed him out
You sang my song, and I too, came out!
Under your gaze the cold is past
My hands reached out to yours
The rays that reached my soul
We danced, you held me close
My head is now full
With hopes and dreams in bloom
I know you cannot stay!
You must leave soon
For now I am content
I vow to enjoy each day!
And for your return, I always pray....

By Sonia Lopez
April 1, 2013

"Captive"

From deep in sleep
I bolted up, with sweat pouring down my
    back
My heart was racing
Was it a dream?
Or did I hear?
A mournful cry, a wretched sound!
It woke me up, it sounded near
I headed towards it
It seemed to come from a road that winds
I had to know what made that sound
The road sign read two miles to town
If I could not find out at least the walk
    would ease my mind
And clear my thoughts, so I headed out!

Down the road not often traveled
On a weeping willow branch, a song rang
    out
Was this the sound?
A lonesome dove sang a song for a love
    not found
It was kind of what I heard,
But more tortured, more profound

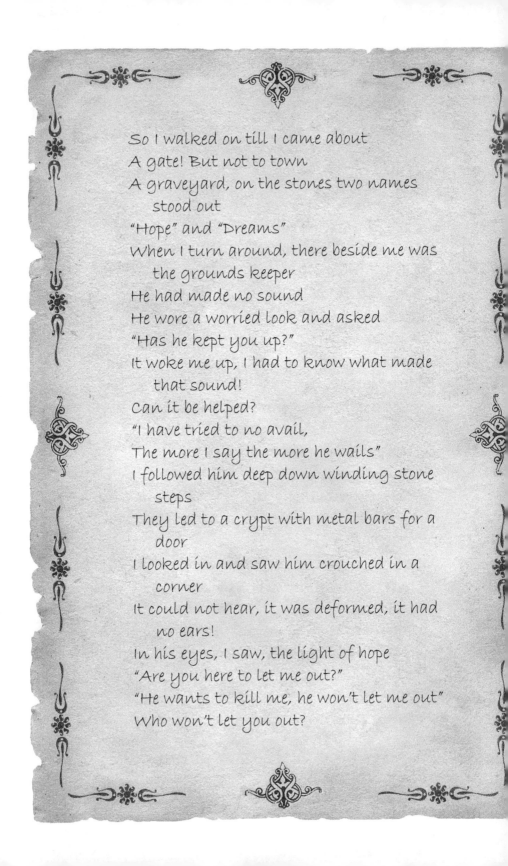

So I walked on till I came about
A gate! But not to town
A graveyard, on the stones two names
    stood out
"Hope" and "Dreams"
When I turn around, there beside me was
    the grounds keeper
He had made no sound
He wore a worried look and asked
"Has he kept you up?"
It woke me up, I had to know what made
    that sound!
Can it be helped?
"I have tried to no avail,
The more I say the more he wails"
I followed him deep down winding stone
    steps
They led to a crypt with metal bars for a
    door
I looked in and saw him crouched in a
    corner
It could not hear, it was deformed, it had
    no ears!
In his eyes, I saw, the light of hope
"Are you here to let me out?"
"He wants to kill me, he won't let me out"
Who won't let you out?

"Reason" and pointed at the grounds
    man
"He says I cannot fly, but I have wings"
He turned but scars was all I saw
He had been torn!
With a sigh I realized I knew the sound!
It is the mournful cry,
The wretched sound
Of a love crazed heart
That has been locked up
And to love, not been allowed!

CPSIA information can be obtained at www.ICGtesting.com
Printed in the USA
BVOW11s2329310315

394131BV00007BA/16/P